D1810827

The Risk in Risk Management

Banks take very large risks by consistently herding in the same perilous directions while believing they are safe and unique. This book presents a risk management framework to understand conformity and deviance within investment banks and other large organizations. It suggests that some groups understand the dynamics of this conformity to their advantage. This requires a deeper understanding of the risk in risk management. Fraudsters can game the system to their advantage legally and illegally; therefore risk managers must understand the interplay of multiple logics in order to govern and manage risk.

Featuring short illustrative cases of massive risk mismanagement, this book walks the reader through four risk management perspectives (economic, institutional, evolutionary, and contrarian) that explain why and how economic rationality is overridden by social forces. By understanding conformity and deviance, groups within organizations will be better equipped to manage risk and go against the tides of conformity to their advantage.

Gregory B. Vit, Ph.D. is Associate Professor (Clinical) of Strategy and Organization at McGill University's Desautels Faculty of Management where he teaches Strategy, Managing Innovation, and Entrepreneurship. Professor Vit's industry experience spans three decades and includes working as Vice President with the Bank of America's Global Corporate and Investment Banking Group where he specialized in international capital raising and corporate finance. He also worked as a financier in sales and structuring at TD Securities Inc.'s Capital Markets and Derivative Products Group Desk. Professor Vit is also director of the Dobson Centre for Entrepreneurial Studies at McGill University where he continues to research and write about entrepreneurial financial fraudsters within large organizations.

The Risk in Risk Management

Financial Organizations & the Problem of Conformity

Gregory B. Vit

Routledge
Taylor & Francis Group

NEW YORK AND LONDON

First published 2013
by Routledge
711 Third Avenue, New York, NY 10017

Simultaneously published in the UK
by Routledge
2 Park Square, Milton Park, Abingdon, Oxon OX14 4RN

Routledge is an imprint of the Taylor & Francis Group, an informa business

© 2013 Taylor & Francis

The right of Gregory B. Vit to be identified as author of this work has been asserted by him in accordance with sections 77 and 78 of the Copyright, Designs and Patents Act 1988.

All rights reserved. No part of this book may be reprinted or reproduced or utilized in any form or by any electronic, mechanical, or other means, now known or hereafter invented, including photocopying and recording, or in any information storage or retrieval system, without permission in writing from the publishers.

Trademark notice: Product or corporate names may be trademarks or registered trademarks, and are used only for identification and explanation without intent to infringe.

Library of Congress Cataloging-in-Publication Data
Vit, Gregory B.
The risk in risk management : financial organizations & the problem of conformity / Gregory B. Vit.
p. cm.
Includes bibliographical references and index.
1. Financial institutions–Risk management–Case studies. 2. Banks and banking–Risk management–Case studies. 3. Financial services industry–Risk management–Case studies. 4. Risk management–Case studies. I. Title.
HG173.V538 2013
332.1068'1–dc23
2012033558

ISBN: 978-0-415-50984-8 (hbk)
ISBN: 978-0-415-50985-5 (pbk)
ISBN: 978-0-203-12461-1 (ebk)

Typeset in Berling
by Keystroke, Station Road, Codsall, Wolverhampton

SUSTAINABLE FORESTRY INITIATIVE
Certified Sourcing
www.sfiprogram.org
SFI-00555
The SFI label applies to the text stock.

Printed and bound in the United States of America by Walsworth Publishing Company, Marceline, MO.

This work is dedicated to Tey, Alexander and Nico with my faithful thanks for their thoughts and encouragement.

Thanks

I also wish to thank Maddy, Saanen and Ella for their helpful comments.

Contents

Foreword

The Risk in Risk Management

An entire finance industry exists to predict the unpredictable. We call it Wall Street. We read analysts' reports, scrutinize credit ratings and eyeball stock price charts looking for answers to insoluble problems. We build legitimacy and attribute success to good decisions by individuals and blame the environment and organizations for bad results. Under these two accounts of reality we are either subjects freely acting on the world or objects being acted upon with few degrees of freedom.

The Risk Manager's Paradox

Banks take very large risks by consistently herding in the same perilous directions while paradoxically believing that they are safe and unique. Why and how is this so? This is an important question that has not been addressed by most books written about professional organizations and investment banks, which are either micro-economic in nature, prescriptive heroic accounts of success, or catastrophic accounts of failure.

This book uniquely presents a framework that uses four different packages of constructs and logics to understand conformity and deviance within investment banks and other large organizations.

It will, for the first time, assemble different case studies of risk mismanagement. By walking the reader through different yet complementary conceptual perspectives on risk, the book might explain why and how economic rationality is overridden by social forces.

Every large organization believes it is unique and can make strategic choices, yet it often herds in the same direction as its peers. Tremendous pressures of conformity exist. In this volume, I have tried to understand *why* banks are full of very clever people that consistently engage in conformist actions that often do not make economic sense. In fact, this blind conformity can be dangerous.

It is possible that some groups manage to understand the dynamics of this conformity and go against them to their advantage. This may require a deep understanding of the risk in risk management. Fraudsters can game the system to their advantage legally and illegally; therefore risk managers must understand multiple logics in order to govern and manage risk.

I propose a framework that demonstrates that most organizations can improve their understanding of risk by taking a more holistic view. This has important theoretical, societal and managerial relevance.

The academic treatment of risk in the risk and strategy literature that is often adopted by banks and management consultants views the organization as a subject that decides how to be different. Many critiques of economic rationality have underlined that these modernist strategy prescriptions have zero predictive power and actually result in convergence of thought and action. At the opposite end of the academic spectrum are "institutionalists" who argue that organizations are objects with few degrees of freedom. For example, investment banks may be viewed as institutional fortresses that are protected by and protect their embedded positions. Thus, multiple views can be used to describe conformity. The purpose of this volume is not to abandon reason, current risk management practices or economic logic. Rather, its purpose is to illustrate how economic rationality must be combined with a more holistic understanding of risk management.

I have collected a series of essays that I have written on this topic for this volume and believe that it is best suited for those that have a general interest in the management of risk in organizations. In many cases, they have been adapted and rewritten to appeal to a wider audience beyond the academic world.

Gregory B. Vit, McGill University
February 2013

Acknowledgments

Chapter 3: Based on Vit, G. (1996). Financial Services Industry Mismanagement. *International Journal of Service Industry Management*, 7 (3), 6–16, and reprinted by permission of author, all rights reserved.

Chapter 4: Based on Vit, G. (2007). The Multiple Logics of Conformity and Contrarianism: The Problem with Investment Banks and Bankers. The final, definitive version of this paper has been published in the *Journal of Management Inquiry*, 16 (3), September 2007, 217–226 by SAGE Publications, Inc. All rights reserved ©.

Chapter 5: Based on Vit, G. (2006). Organizational Conformity and Contrarianism: Regular Irregular Trading at National Australia Bank. *Corporate Governance*, 6 (2), 203–214, and reprinted by permission of author, all rights reserved.

Chapter 6: Based on Vit, G. (2010). Competing Logics: Project Failure in Gaspesia. *European Management Journal*, doi: 10.1016/j.emj.2010.10. 003, ©2010 Elsevier Ltd. All rights reserved.

Chapter 8: Partly based on Vit, G. (2009). Foreseeing the Problem of Conformity in Strategy Teaching, Research and Practice. In B. MacKay and L. Constanza (eds.) *The Handbook of Research on Strategy and Foresight*. Northampton, MA: Edward Elgar Publishing Limited, 518–527. Reprinted by permission from author with major editing, all rights reserved.

Chapter 1

The Problem of Conformity in Financial Organizations

The stock market crash of 2008 is an interesting example of the override of numbers and economic logic in and around an unexpected financial shock. Although dramatic and recent, similar underlying social processes that eclipse numbers have existed in previous excesses since the beginning of banking and continue to prevail.

This book, using case studies for illustrative purposes, will seek to explain why many large financial organizations, full of seemingly rational individuals, were defrauded by large bets that did not make organizational economic sense. It will discuss how social sense was managed and mismanaged by numerate practitioners, before and after the taking of massive financial provisions and write-downs.

More specifically this book presents four alternative risk models that seek to explain how these very risky bets happened. They are the dominant and mainly quantitative risk analysis (quant) model, the contrarian model, the evolutionary model, and the institutional structure model. These risk management models shed light upon the non-economic activities of rainmaking quant in-groups that engaged in large and costly speculation in opaque and highly risky "investments." This is further reinforced at higher levels of analysis by a mimetic institutional field and the boom phase of an economic cycle. Many of the principal actors who suffered heavy losses in these case studies ostensibly responded to quantitative analyses by betting upon so-called innovative displacements and applied quantitative financial models. This book outlines how the rules, cognitive routines and ideological pressures of an institutional environment and systemic mania wove together to eclipse the technical and economic rationality of risk governors within these organizations. This abdication and override of technical rationality, fraudulently masquerading as innovation and risk management, is explored.

Retrospective and Prospective Explanations

The recent spectacular and unexpected financial losses of 2008 and other crises (i.e. Latin American debt 1981, US Savings and Loan 1980s and early 1990s, the dot-com bubble of 1999) have shocked many financial institutions to the point of threatening their survival. In hindsight, organizational observers, investors and researchers have pointed to seemingly obvious signs of systemic excess and massive risk taking over time.[1,2] How then is it possible that such large warning signs were either not seen or, alternatively, seen and yet ignored?[3] Also, given the tidal wave of $700 billion in US Treasury financial support (TARP) to the banking system and recent volatility in financial markets, what, if anything, is different now? Chapter 2 helps us understand how numbers were, are and will continue to be manipulated by proposing four alternative risk management models that, when combined, form the Holistic Risk Management Model (HRMM). It is exploratory in nature. This book will focus upon processes within cases of risk taking that resulted in large runaway losses for financial institutions and the failure to detect the massive legal and illegal bets. For the most part, the illustrative cases involve substantial risk taking by rainmaking elites. Although retrospective accounts provide 20/20 hindsight, I wish to underline processes that can be applied prospectively. For example, presciently (or coincidentally), in 2006 some observers raised significant doubts about the opacity of numbers, bogus transactions, and synchronicity, that also were apparent in the crash of 2008, at various levels of analysis such as in-house trading groups, investment banks, the banking industry and the economy. This is outlined in Chapter 4.

The Override of Numbers: A Dynamic View

When viewing a financial crisis in hindsight and in foresight, there are two important packages of logics and processes that become apparent at an organizational level of analysis. These processes lead to two important outcomes (Events 1 and 2). The first is the accumulation of risky activities by employees within a group of insiders, of an organization, which at some point secretly "bets the farm" or threatens the survival of an organization. Somehow the economic rationality and control of internal and external risk governors using mainly quantitative models is undermined and overridden (see Figure 1.1). The second event is when management and related parties realize that there is a dire problem on hand. This results in the recognition of large existing or potential losses, and often causes a credit, liquidity and confidence crisis. This may even end in a firm's demise and bankruptcy, sale to a more solid acquirer, a bail-out by government, or some combination thereof. Given the synchronous nature of most large financial institutions and markets, imitative behavior at a higher industry or institutional field level of analysis may occur. When this happens, the sum of many of the same processes and assumptions within organizations within an industry and institutional field can add up to big problems.

I have compressed these two processes, bubble building and bubble bursting, into two discrete events (Event 1 and Event 2) for illustrative purposes. Within an organization, first there is a period of sustained success by a quantitative products in-group based upon knowingly taking large risks (and a focus upon revenue growth and cash flow irrespective

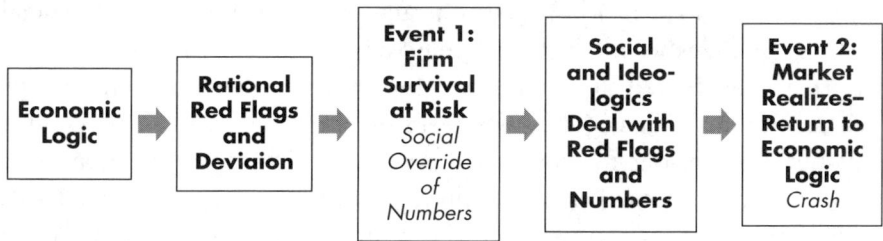

FIGURE 1.1 The Dynamics of the Social Override of Numbers and a Crash: Events 1 and 2

of this risk) that is not completely understood by internal and/or external risk governors. The magnitude of risks taken eventually reaches a point whereby hidden losses threaten the survival of the firm. Next, red flags and seemingly obvious facts (often numerical) warn that the system is at risk. These warning signs are ignored by risk governors and denied by risk takers. This decoupling of economic and technical rationality and its override by social forces drive revenues and asset prices even higher. Adam Smith calls this "over-trading."[4] Although a careful look at numbers and fundamental analyses may tell a different story, a highly profitable fictive quantitative model/money machine is hailed by quant insiders as having been found. I call this Event 1 *Social Override*.

The focus of this book is on how non-economic social logics deal with the seemingly obvious massive red flags thrown up by a risk management system's economic and technical warnings. Eventually there is the collective realization by a consensus of managerial and market participants that there is a clear absence of numerate technical/economic rationality behind asset price gains and a return to assumptions of technical rationality (and an examination of numbers and their attendant assumptions), which then results in financial collapse. I call this Event 2 *Crash*. The logics leading up to Event 1 and Event 2 are the focus of this volume. Illegal deception is fraud, while the intentional legal override of economic logic is innocent fraud.[5]

Two Events: Social Override of Numbers and Crash

It follows that if social decoupling and override can be better understood by examining logics and processes around these events, future financial bubbles and crashes might be mollified or avoided by risk governors (or, alternatively, fueled and exploited by manipulative quant in-groups within organizations). The bubble reinforces conformity and creates favorable conditions for contrarian deviation and fraudulent activity.[6,7] In the cases discussed in this volume, contrarian in-groups used this social space and numerous processes in order to deviate and profit from conformist processes. Often, opaque quantitative models provided to analysts and debt rating agencies further catalyzed the process.

Cheerleaders and Models

Since the crash of 2008, much has been written about the inherent inappropriateness of David Li's Gaussian copula formula's application to the pricing of tranches in the credit default swap market, which resulted in silk purse AAA ratings being created from sow-ear bad mortgage loans. For example, the US Government's Financial Crisis Inquiry Report (FCIR) notes that "of all mortgage backed securities it had rated AAA in 2006, Moody's downgraded 76% to Junk."[8]

Post-crash scrutiny reveals that the lower boundary condition of the complex valuation models used flawed assumptions such as a constant recovery assumption of 75 percent of bad mortgages that may have trumped other model parameters such as expected default rates and correlations and resulted in AAA ratings for large tranches of packaged "junk" securities.

For example, the FCIR notes that Moody's credit ratings of packages of junk (sub-prime mortgages) were based upon three main mathematical models that were meant to produce credit ratings (AAA = most credit worthy, etc.) that would allow investors to compare across other asset classes and time.[9] Investors relied upon credit ratings despite disclaimers buried in prospectuses saying that ratings are solely statements of opinion (this is analogous to the disclaimers found in business school cases that disclaim that cases are intended only for teaching purposes, but not as an example of how to manage . . .). Furthermore, in testimony to Congressional investigators, a former head of Moody's sub-prime rating department noted massive inconsistencies in their rational analytic approach and that quantitative analysis, although flawed, was eclipsed by qualitative considerations: "One common misperception is that credit ratings are derived solely from a mathematical process . . . Ultimately, ratings are subjective opinions that reflect the majority of the (rating) committee's members."[10]

Curiously, Moody's and the other major rating agencies (Standard & Poor's and Fitch) appear not to have legal liability regarding the accuracy of their ratings since courts have ruled that they are de facto immune to prosecution. They have also been deemed to be merely exercising their right to free speech under the first amendment of the US Constitution, although this may be contested.[11] Thus credit ratings belong to the magical potions of management such as financial forecasting, market research and capital budgeting, that build legitimacy, reduce uncertainty and endeavor to predict the unpredictable.[12,13] It is also very interesting to note, in the context of the cornering of the junk bond market and subsequent Milliken prosecution, that numbers related to junk bonds have been manipulated and misrepresented as being a money machine and safe in the past.[14]

Discourse is used to build legitimacy as artifacts and texts such as "bad loans" not "bad bankers" are blamed and infused with value and causality.

Chapter 2

The Holistic Risk Management Model (HRMM)

Understanding Multiple Logics: Economic, Social and Ideological

The observations of risk managers, boards of directors, bank examiners and other observers that unfold in this book point to the override of economic rationality by ideological and social logics as outlined in Figure 2.1. The Holistic Risk Management Model's (HRMM) basic premise is that a combination of different and powerful views of risk management can be used to explain why large organizations that are full of clever people often do silly things. These are shown in the quadrants of Figure 2.1.

Numerous economic-rational red flags existed in most of the cases discussed in this book. Quadrant 1 represents the dominant rational economic risk management model that most banks utilize. Subsequent chapters will highlight the cases of banks that were at the forefront of quant-rational risk management, such as National Bank of Australia, UBS and Société Générale (SocGen), and how their systems were overridden by other non-economic logics. Parmalat's bankers, National Bank of Australia, UBS and SocGen all relied upon sophisticated mathematical models and micro-processes to control risk via quantitative and rational risk models. This process is Cartesian as risks are anticipated, and rules are created to manage and to flag breaches and deviations from the norm.[1] Figure 2.2 outlines these rational risk management processes.[2]

*Risk Governor Understanding of
Non-Economic Logics*

	Quadrant 1	Quadrant 3
High	Quant-Rational RM analysis → rules control/ create → optimal events	Contrarian RM events → manipulation/ deviation
	Quadrant 4	**Quadrant 2**
Low	Evolutionary RM chance and incumbency → suboptimal events	Institutional RM social structure → events or inertia

*Risk Governor
Understanding
of Economic
Logics*

                         Low   **High**

FIGURE 2.1 The Holistic Risk Management Model (HRMM)

Source: Vit (2006; 2007; 2009)

    This dominant risk management model is mechanistic and prescriptive. The model assumes that rigorous internal and external analysis is ongoing, that this in turn results in optimal rules, decisions and action. It assumes a high degree of technical and economic rationality and predictability. Routines are put in place to manage risk.[3]

    I have noted that there exist implicit assumptions behind this model that should be made explicit. First, the model is highly prescriptive. It assumes that if senior managers exclusively use a highly quantitative model, they will be more successful than those who do not. Second, the model assumes that the top managers within organizations can have a significant impact on their domain and are subjects that anticipate,

FIGURE 2.2 Quant-Rational Risk Management

Source: Vit (2009)

analyze, decide and optimize. They are assumed to be able to create successful strategies and act upon the world so as to significantly change it. Success may be attributed to this activity, yet may be unrelated to it, as discussed in the alternative models presented below. Third, numbers, financial models and large volumes of hard data are relied upon, and strategies are codified, aggregated and formalized. Soft data, holistic approaches and intuition are excluded. Fourth, the model is temporal-centric, or assumed to be the most advanced to date, even though similar approaches have existed over the last century, and USA-centric as it is often espoused by US business schools and US consultants.[4]

Numbers, rationality and quantification are necessary but not suf-ficient to manage risk since strong corporate culture and mindless organizational routines, habits and patterns of behaviour often trump this economic logic. They are represented in Figure 1.1 as non-economic risk management and mismanagement leading up to an Event 1 (social override of economic data) and Event 2 (crash).

Alternative Risk Management Models

The figures below present alternative risk management models.[5] At a larger level of analysis, the institutional risk management model in Figure 2.3 (and Quadrant 2 of Figure 2.1) suggests that, contrary to rational risk management assumptions of analysis and rules driving optimizing organizational action as seen in Figure 2.2, the weight of social structure within an organization and particularly its industry and broader institutional environment creates its own action and inaction. Invisible institutional processes trump markets and models. For example, I illustrate institutional RM in a later chapter. Canadian banks took bil-lions of dollars in write-downs of Latin American debt in the early 1980s and may have avoided the US debt crisis in 2008 due to an institutional fortress enjoyed within Canada. Vit and Graham observed that the top five Canadian banks held approximately 85 percent of the Canadian bank market in the 1880s and the 1990s, and that this is still the case today even with more open borders to foreign banks.[6,7]

Large institutional structure can also have negative consequences. The same institutional risk management logic treated at an organizational and

social structure ➔ events or non-events

FIGURE 2.3 Institutional Risk Management

Source: Vit (2009)

industry level of analysis in Canada can be applied to a global level of analysis that is reinforcing. For example, within the investment banking industry, external legitimacy is built and institutions are fortified by management consultants, bond rating agencies, auditors, industry associations and journals, which assist at arriving at Event 1, the social override of economic risk management. Insight about economic risk management within one organization may not be sufficient to understand the institutional complexity of an entire institutional system.[8] Counter-intuitively, one organization trying to reduce risk, such as SocGen trying to sell off large unauthorized trader positions, on an aggregate level, may actually increase systemic risk. This was the fear over Bear Stearns' insolvency and Lehman's bankruptcy. Numbers, models and risk exposures within banks are complex and private, so that no one has a pre-crash insight into the entire system, including regulatory officials. This represents a significant and complex challenge, which is further aggravated by an even larger level of analysis: where we are in an economic cycle.

Evolutionary risk management illustrated in Figure 2.4 (and also in Quadrant 4 of Figure 2.1) suggests that many small chance events may contribute to eventual quantum change, and that micro-routines and habits are obstacles to adaptation until an organization is faced with a big crisis.[9] For example, subsequent chapters will demonstrate how risk governors did not have a firm economic or social understanding of runaway losses. They were locked into their narrowly defined incumbent routines, and many small chance events resulted in the opportunity for manipulation, leading to heavy losses for the Gaspesia paper project and the National Bank of Australia's foreign exchange trading room.

FIGURE 2.4 Evolutionary Risk Management

Source: Vit (2009)

Contrarian risk management, featured in Quadrant 3 of Figure 2.1, suggests that some individuals and groups have a holistic understanding of economic, institutional and evolutionary risk management processes. This allows them to take a contrarian view and use the economic, institutional and evolutionary processes found in the other quadrants and figures above to their advantage. This may represent a holistic risk manager's steadfast refusal to do a seemingly attractive deal or, on the other side of the coin, a legal or illegal fraudster's skill in getting a dodgy deal done.

For example, contrarian risk management, illustrated in Figure 2.5, can be used to explain bets by in-groups of proprietary traders that lead to an Event 1 situation. In a booming market, highly complex quantitative models such as junk bond default models become the conventional wisdom.[10] Traders will take on disguised but increasing levels of risk that will produce large increasing returns that are attributed to these money machine quantitative models and processes. Since SocGen likely did not plan to lose €4.9 billion in trading derivatives, or UBS its $53 billion in write-offs (e.g. nor did UBS and JP Morgan plan their recent losses in London, nor did the SEC plan to exonerte Madoff 10 times or Lehman to be bankrupted), the contrarian model is applicable to risk governors and risk fraudsters (legal and illegal) throughout the build-up to Events 1 and 2. Retrospectively, the plethora of ex-post reports, discursive strategies and action plans that are cited in this volume are evidence of the use of social processes to shape events via attribution to factors seemingly outside the control of risk governors—a push to explain with the logics of Quadrants 4 and 2 in Figure 2.1. Prospectively, I argue that an awareness of the dynamics of the logics presented in the three quadrants that is represented by contrarian Quadrant 3 will improve a risk manager's ability to conceptualize holistic risk as well as quantitative measures of financial risk.

For example, Quadrant 3 of Figure 2.1, from the perspective of legal and illegal fraudsters at National Australia Bank, UBS, SocGen and

event → manipulation/deviation

FIGURE 2.5 Contrarian Risk Management

Source: Vit (2009)

Parmalat, represents an in-group's contrarian insight into all logics that may be necessary to override red flags produced by technical rationality between Event 1 and Event 2. It suggests that this awareness and understanding of fraudulent contrarians should also exist on the part of risk governors in the build-ups to Events 1 and 2. It further implies that risk governors must understand not only the technical efficiency of their processes, systems and economic logics, but also their unwritten social practices, internal and external social logics that were manipulated extensively by traders and fraudsters between Events 1 and 2. Quadrant 4 of Figure 2.1 presents an alternative risk management view that suggests that risk governor ignorance of both economic rationality and social and ideological pressures may allow small chance events and the Riemann sum of many small meaningless organizational routines to combine to create big suboptimal events such as a fraud (Parmalat) or trading excesses (National Australia Bank and SocGen), and huge risk positions (UBS and SocGen) that could threaten the survival of an organization. For example, armies of managers at National Australia Bank, SocGen and UBS were locked in their day-to-day algorithmic micro-routines and not concerned with massive notional volumes being put on by traders in proprietary trading groups (UBS) or outright consistent evidence of fraud (National Australia Bank, SocGen). Palmer and Maher have suggested that the US mortgage meltdown fits with a Normal Accident explanation since the US mortgage market was a tightly coupled and complex technological system.[11] Perrow disagrees, suggesting that the meltdown was not an accident, and nor was it due to institutionalism, but rather that it has more to do with endogenous reasons related to key agents who knew what they were doing.[12]

Conclusion

The recent social economic research on the crash of 2008 is retrospective. Yet, I argue here that not much has changed regarding the underlying dynamics of the build-up to another prospective crash. Having tracked the birth and evolution of risk management failures within larger risk management systems, organizations, and a broader institutional and systemic context, I note that only a handful of individuals have gone to jail, to date, for criminal excesses related to the 2008 crash. Apart from tinkering with capital, compensation and the creation of weak legislation that results in the increased employment of armies of accounting graduates, consultants and lawyers to produce yet more governance checklists (Quadrant 1, Figure 2.1), the battle between contrarian fraudsters and risk managers continues. The Holistic Risk Management Model proposed in Figure 2.1 suggests that multiple logics can be combined at multiple levels of analysis. This would help explain how and why small influential groups such as risk governors and quant traders can create superficial certainty and legitimacy regarding the future outcomes of massive speculation in products and markets that are highly uncertain, risky and impenetrable. The HRMM has sought to demonstrate that the same risk management logics that promote critical thought and judgment within risk management systems can also be used to explain processes that resulted in the decoupling of numbers and economic rationality, and large blind bets that overrode the technical rationality of conventional machine bureaucracy bank risk management systems and risk management processes.

An important contribution of the HRMM is that different under-standings of these multiple logics may be gained from viewing them in relation to different processes as summarized in Figure 2.1 and sub-sequent figures. The cases presented in the chapters of this book will demonstrate that, rather than being idiosyncratic and isolated incidents of indefensible fraud and innocent fraud, many risk governors decoupled from the underlying technical and economic logic of these organizations intentionally and unintentionally.[13]

The financial organizations' histories, positions in their environments, and the unintended consequences of the actions of participants are evidence of a veneer of economic rationality. The unique non-economic logics of the major and minor risk governors drove their aspirations and the frauds forward, as will be discussed. Facts were heavily filtered and selected by risk managers' appreciative systems.[14,15,16] The limited identification of most risk governors with their own non-economic logics created sense throughout the frauds as their aspirations eclipsed eco-nomic warning signs between Events 1 and 2.[17,18]

The HRMM and case studies to follow will be of particular interest and importance to risk managers/governors within large financial service organizations and to scholars and students of risk management. An understanding of the Holistic Risk Management Model is a first step to avoiding potentially enormous future social and economic losses.

Chapter 3

Institutional Risk Management

Case 1: The Canadian Banking Paradigm

Chapter Summary

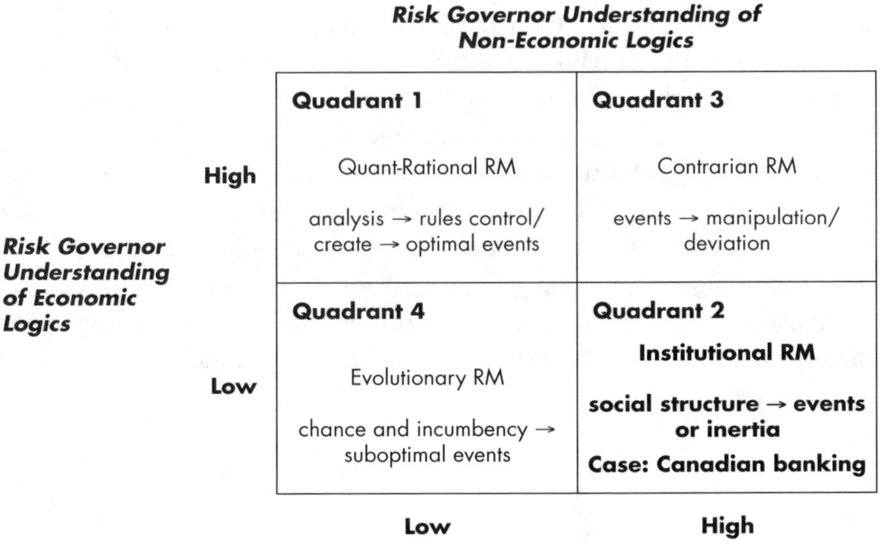

Risk Governor Understanding of Non-Economic Logics

		Low	High
Risk Governor Understanding of Economic Logics	**High**	**Quadrant 1** Quant-Rational RM analysis → rules control/ create → optimal events	**Quadrant 3** Contrarian RM events → manipulation/ deviation
	Low	**Quadrant 4** Evolutionary RM chance and incumbency → suboptimal events	**Quadrant 2** **Institutional RM** **social structure → events or inertia** **Case: Canadian banking**

FIGURE 3.1 The Holistic Risk Management Model (HRMM)

Source: Vit (2009)

Institutionalists argue that banks will likely not change unless faced with a big crisis. The following text was written almost two decades ago. Some Canadian banking laws have changed, yet Canadian banking remains highly institutionalized. Canadian pension funds can now invest internationally, leverage is conservatively capped by regulators, deposits are insured up to $100,000, and the single legal person ownership rule was increased to 30 percent per legal person, thus still preventing takeovers. Also, Canadian banks are for the most part non-unionized and continue to dominate the Canadian retail, commercial and investment banking capital markets. The institutional fortress is alive and well. In the chapter below, I write about the dangers of an overly ossified industry. In it I note that more than one hundred years ago the five largest Canadian banks made up a vast majority of the Canadian Banking market and this is still the case today. The oligopoly that is Canadian banking is described in this chapter as an "institutional fortress." As it was in the 1920s, most recently this has been very advantageous to Canadian banks as they did not get involved in the 2008 sub-prime credit disaster, in which many foreign banks did. This was due to blind luck or prescience.

Although our teaching and textbooks are dominated by assumptions of near perfect markets and free, pure competitiveness, many, if not most, industries are not. For example, an oligopolistic nature is not the exclusive province of banks, as many Canadian industries are dominated by large players that can be counted on one hand, such as railways, telcos, major beer companies, national hockey league teams and so on.

Thus, invisible institutional fortresses are everywhere, and an understanding of visible and invisible norms is very important in risk management as they can influence the taking or avoidance of large risks. The following chapter traces the history of Canadian banking and demonstrates that an institutional approach adds another important institutional lens to the Holistic Risk Management Model through which to view risk.

Financial Service Industry Mismanagement: Institutionalization and Conformist Strategy[1]

Institutional theory examines the relationship between an organization and its broader institutional context. As organizations within well-institutionalized sectors get ossified, the attention of management shifts from efficient management of internal processes to effective mismanagement. By this we mean that the forces of legitimacy and conformity active in the institutional environment can be most powerful and result in dangerous or potentially risky conformist strategy.

DiMaggio and Powell call the institutional process by which organizations become homogeneous and resemble each other "isomorphism."[2] The authors distinguish between three forms of isomorphism:

> (1) Coercive isomorphism that stems from political influence and the problem of legitimacy; (2) mimetic isomorphism resulting from imitation and standard responses to uncertainty; and (3) normative isomorphism, associated with professionalization.[3]

Although these categories are not mutually exclusive, the authors provide interesting insight into the behavior of bureaucratized institutions. They find it paradoxical that the more these organizations try to be innovative, the more they resemble each other on an aggregate basis, since they are all changing in the same direction. Other observers also point to the dangers of superficial rationality.[4,5,6,7,8,9,10,11,12] This has been apparent in the field of management itself, where critics have emphasized the need for alternative process-oriented or descriptive research.[13,14,15] Alvesson notes that organizations, including consulting firms, universities, businesses and publications, have in some cases institutionalized rational and prescriptive models that focus on atomistic, micro-economic concepts of an organization.[16]

Thus, the institutional perspective can be most powerful in debunking various myths of rationality and so-called scientific management. Research by Covalski and Dirsmith on a service industry application – a university – illustrates this point.[17] In this situation, the University of Wisconsin did not conform to the social norms and acceptable behavior expected by the state. Even the state's governor was involved with the rejection of the university's new budgetary approach. Again, the underlying theme developed by the authors is the importance of the institutional environment:

> This acceptable discourse, such as budgeting, is always an intrinsic part of some social situation; it is never an independent instrument or simply a tool for description and institutionalization. Although this language is cloaked in the appearance of objectivity and neutrality, it is ultimately directed toward establishing and maintaining hierarchies of authority and status. Power relationships and the reproduction of the control structure are to be found in the uneventful routines of organizational life.[18]

Zucker has contributed significantly to the formalization of institutional theory by proposing two approaches that highlight the dichotomy between institutionalization at the organizational level (organization as institution) and institutionalization outside the organization (environment as institution).[19] Zucker notes that a dominant theme in institutional theory is that the environment, and principally the state, pressures organizations to conform in order to retain legitimacy and improve their chances of survival. This results in ceremonial or mythical behavior that is often divorced from the technical and efficiency-driven activities of the organization.

Most institutional theorists agree that an understanding of shared values or "appreciative systems" and relationships is critical. One of the common central tenets of institutional theory is that powerful and potentially dysfunctional pressures of conformity exist between institutions.[20] The institutional fortress framework presented below provides a new conceptual framework in which the dynamics of legitimacy building mismanagement are treated.

The Institutional Fortress Model of Mismanagement

Isomorphism exists when organizations are homogeneous and behave similarly and is related to an organization's internal perspective, and its external position within its institutional environment. Building on Thompson's input, process and output activities approach, a well-ensconced firm within a protected industry may be viewed as an organization that is protected within invisible walls or norms that we call an "institutional fortress," as outlined in Figure 3.2 below.[21] The case of Canadian banks is used to illustrate this idea in the next section of this chapter; however, any highly institutionalized industry will have similar walls and gateways.

Walls are erected around key inputs such as raw materials, capital, technology or labor.[22,23,24] Formal laws or informal practices also protect outputs. This may take the form of exclusive market, geographic or product franchises. Organizations within the fortress are essentially money machines provided that the institutional context, or wall of the fortress,

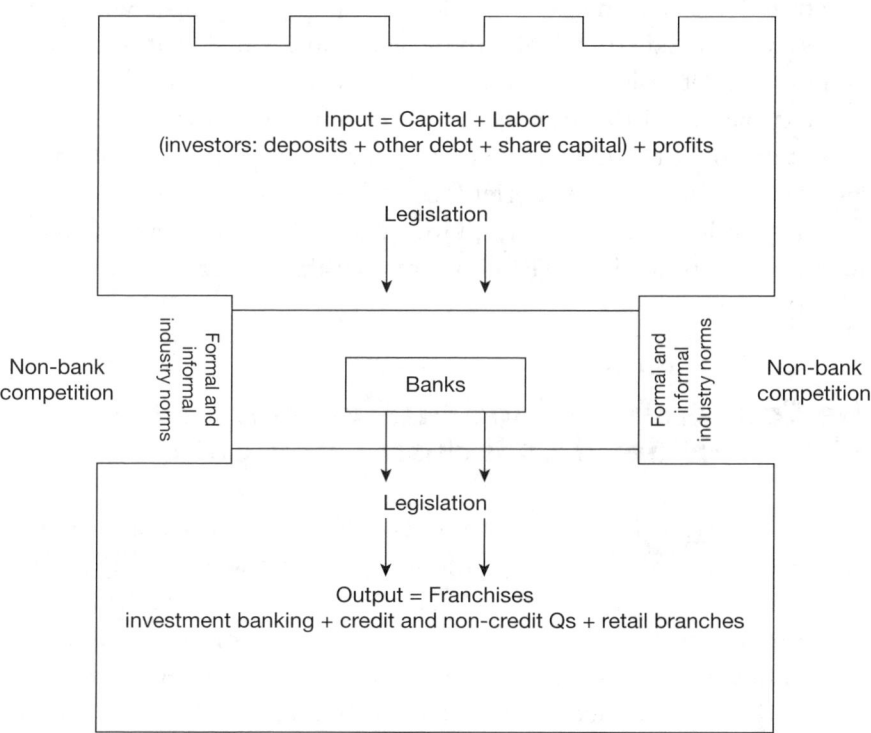

FIGURE 3.2 Institutional Fortress

Source: Vit (1996)

is stable. With age, the walls normally get thicker and taller. The organizations within them become less concerned with external enemies (economic and competitive forces) and eventually cannot or will not see them. Thus, "court activity" within the fortress becomes routine (rigid structure) and turns away from the efficient allocation of scarce resources as they are relatively abundant. Instead, the organization focuses on ritual and ceremony. Wall maintenance outside the fortress is achieved by legitimacy-building activities.

Effectiveness is more important than efficiency, as the maintenance of ancient walls (protected inputs and outputs) supersedes in importance the efficiency of those within this task environment.[25] Thompson calls this "buffering and smoothing," and institutional theorists refer to this process as the "decoupling" of efficiency and the promulgation of "myths." We call this "mismanagement."[26,27,28] Given this comfortable and attractive arrangement, it would seem likely that those within the fortress would like to remain there and those outside it should be clamoring to get inside. This is the dictate of isomorphism.[29,30]

The dynamics of the architecture and evolution of the fortress walls are best illustrated by examining their social construction longitudinally. The next section provides a brief financial services industry application of the institutional fortress concept by tracking the nature, evolution and emergence of powerful invisible norms within the Canadian banking industry.

The Canadian Banking Institutional Fortress: A Financial Services Industry Application

Figure 3.2 is typical of the institutional system or fortress of Canadian banking. The rules that governed the system were and are highly institutionalized with key dependencies protected by the state and the banking industry. The industry was, and still is, highly concentrated since the six largest Canadian banks control over 90 percent of total bank assets.[31]

The primary input activity for a bank is securing capital and labor. In Canada, this activity is protected by many laws and regulations that have evolved through historical accident and successful lobbying. For example, the large Canadian banks are insulated from takeover attempts since, by law, ownership by one group, entity or legal person is limited to a maximum of 10 percent of voting shares. Large Canadian institutional investors, such as pension funds and insurance companies, are required by law to invest 80 percent of their assets in Canada. Consequently, the large and stable Canadian banks are a natural haven for this capital. Finally, deposit taking is facilitated since every retail deposit is insured for up to $60,000 by the federal government's federal deposit insurance corporation for financial institutions. Thus, although not guaranteed, capital input activities are significantly buffered by existing legislation. The bank task and technical environments are virtually identical, with most banks offering the same products and services at similar costs. In addition, banks have been successful in avoiding the unionization of their large workforces, thus retaining control over labor input.[32,33] The laws governing banks are illustrated in Figure 3.2 as walls, which channel and protect inputs. Banks have control of some of these gateways and little control over others. Notwithstanding, it is argued here that the overall impact of this institutional environment is most beneficial to banks.

The main output activities of the banks are also protected by laws and institutional arrangements that in many cases are exclusive product and market franchises. For example, until recently Canadian banking and investment dealer (e.g. stock brokering) businesses were separated by law. In 1987 the banking laws were changed to permit banks to own securities firms. The large Canadian banks, with the exception of one bank which created its own, promptly bought the major Canadian investment dealers. The end result is that the investment banking business in Canada is dominated by the investment banking subsidiaries of the Canadian banks. The distribution of capital in the form of loans is also facilitated by the extensive branch networks of the major banks. Legislation also opened up the lending output channels for the banks, as discussed below.

Further Defenses: Institutional Arrangements and Norms Within the Canadian Banking Industry

The historical institutional relationship between Canadian banks and the government has been most beneficial to Canadian banks. Over time,

Canadian banks have benefited from the active lobbying of the Canadian Bankers' Association, formal legislation and favorable informal norms as discussed below.

The Canadian Bankers' Association

Darroch's historical analysis of the Canadian banking industry over the last century demonstrates that the industry has successfully lobbied the Canadian government for protected markets and products through formal legislation and informal institutional arrangements.[34] For example, the nature of oligopolistic markets and the founding of the Canadian Bankers' Association in 1891 greatly insulated Canadian banks from competition: "The bankers realized that it was imperative to shape public policy in ways beneficial to the industry and they established The Canadian Bankers' Association (CBA) in 1891 to promote their common interests."[35]

Darroch notes that the banks did come under pressure during the economic depression of the 1930s, when the Social Credit Party called for the nationalization of banks. It appears that the creation of a government central bank, the Bank of Canada, in 1935 was in part due to these pressures as, until that time, banks could issue their own banknotes. Darroch also observes that the banks remained solid during this era:

> The bankers did a good job of convincing legislators that the cautious approach taken by Canadian bankers had lessened the effects of the Depression. Canadian bankers had not lent funds to support reckless speculation, and consequently Canadian banks were not failing. On the other hand, bank failures in the US called the whole financial system into question.[36]

Banks continued as depository institutions that invested the majority of their deposits in safe securities such as government bonds up until the mid-1950s, when legislation was changed to allow banks to take security and lend money in the retail consumer market. The former head of the Canadian Bankers' Association, Robert MacIntosh, called it a hop, skip and jump ahead for the banks:[37]

The hop was the permission to make loans on houses (1954). The skip was permission to make loans on cars (1954 and 1967). The jump was removal of the 6 percent ceiling on bank lending rates (1967) . . . Up to 1954 the banks were the major depository for the public's savings, but not the source of funds for most personal and family borrowing. Bank lending was essentially commercial in nature, with a relatively minor portion of bank assets in personal loans. Then in a series of moves which removed the barriers to lending against the security of houses and cars, Parliament brought the banks into touch with the rapidly expanding middle class in the suburbs and small towns of Canada.[38]

It appears that the Canadian banks were at first very reluctant to make mortgage loans for houses for 25-year terms, since it would result in an asset mismatch with deposits of shorter duration. MacIntosh suggests that the president of the CBA in 1954 reluctantly accepted the banks' agreement with the government to make mortgage money available since they were "quasi-public utilities": "It demonstrates that some bankers shared the view that the profit motivation was somewhat modified by social goals."[39]

Favorable Legislation

Furthermore, since a decennial review of the federal law governing banks, known as the "Bank Act," was written into the legislation in 1871, the banks have managed to protect existing markets by virtue of favorable legislation, and the predisposition of most governments to maintain stability. For example, the Bank of Canada observed that the Bank Act revisions of 1967 forbade the concentration of bank ownership by one individual or group of associated individuals from being more than 10 percent of any class of shares of a bank.[40] It also noted that this requirement that banks be widely held was intended to fend off foreign acquisitions, yet resulted in a restriction of commercial-financial owner-ship ties with other companies: "Although this restriction was introduced to prevent potential takeovers of Canadian banks by non-residents, it also had the effect of preventing significant upstream commercial-financial links."[41] Thus, Canadian banks could not be taken over by foreigners.

Somewhat incidental, yet critically important from an institutional theoretic viewpoint, was the consequence that large Canadian banks did not have to answer to any single large block of shareholders that could vote their management out of office.

Favorable Informal Norms

Behind the formal changes in laws cited above was informal political activity. For the most part, the Canadian government has been historically very supportive of the Canadian banking industry through informal means. As previously discussed, a good illustration of this continued support has been the inability of foreign banks to penetrate the Canadian banking sector. Prior to passing formal legislation barring their ownership of a significant share of the Canadian banking market in 1967, the Canadian government resisted acquisition attempts by major foreign banks. MacIntosh describes the problems encountered during the First National City Bank of New York's (Citibank) acquisition of the Mercantile Bank of Canada in 1963 and the alleged unsuccessful attempt of the Chase Manhattan Bank of New York (Chase) at acquiring a large Canadian bank in 1964.[42] He refers to former prime minister Pearson's memoirs recounting the rejection of overtures made by David Rockefeller, the head of Chase:

> I remember receiving David Rockefeller at dinner one night at Sussex Drive . . . He was hoping to get some control and eventually, I suppose, total control of a Canadian bank, and had already taken steps in that direction. I replied, "Well there is no use in your going any further."[43]

Thus, the existing informal and formal norms and laws governing the behavior of banks in Canada have evolved through successful lobbying and historical accident into a unique, stable and still largely protected market.

The stability and good health of the Canadian banking system have been a major concern of the Canadian federal government over the last century. The former governor of Canada's central bank, John Crow, noted that a balance must exist between bank institutional stability and bank efficiency.[44] His comments reflect arguments in favor of institutional fortress building in the Canadian banking industry:

> In conclusion, let me summarize. The legislative and regulatory changes to the structure of the Canadian financial system over the last two decades have mostly had the objective of promoting efficiency. More recently, considerable interest in Canada and worldwide has focused on the need to maintain soundness, stability and impartiality of the system and its institutions. I think such a rebalance of emphasis is appropriate and fully consistent with achieving further development of an efficient, dynamic, internationally competitive system for Canada. Sustained, efficient operation of our financial system will not be assured without the confidence that comes with a strong commitment to soundness. Any legislative or regulatory changes have to be judged on the basis of this fundamental consideration.

DiMaggio and Powell maintain that large organizations which have existed for a long time in non-perfectly competitive markets will resemble one another.[45] This institutional isomorphism is due to the ability of these organizations to dominate a particular domain of activity or organizational field. At the institutional level, Canadian banks were and are isomorphic. In their quest to be at the cutting edge of banking, Canadian banks have looked more and more similar.

This drive towards innovativeness actually resulted in herding behavior and the loan losses and crises related to Latin American lending, oil and gas lending, leveraged buy-out and real estate lending in recent history.[46] DiMaggio and Powell call this desire to be different a paradox since it results in uniform behavior in the industry.[47] Thus, the aggregate lending behavior of Canadian banks appears to substantiate Meyer and Rowan's claim that the myths and rituals of established and powerful institutions override task and technological efficiency.[48]

Implications for Financial Services Industry Mismanagement

The main implication for financial services industry management is to create an awareness of how and why potentially dangerous mismanagement resulting in conformist strategy exists (e.g. large bank crises and losses to Latin America, leveraged buy-outs, real estate and derivatives) using the institutional fortress model. This model is descriptive rather than prescriptive. It suggests that a historical examination of invisible, socially constructed norms (walls) that form around a sector's inputs and outputs is a powerful level of analysis. This mismanagement within financial service industries is effected and affected by external and internal factors. In contrast to many current management prescriptions, we propose the following as a point of departure for further research into possible explanatory variables that both create and reinforce mismanagement, institutional fortress building and bounded rationality.

External Factors

As illustrated by our discussion of Canadian banking, common institutional norms and shared behavior, or isomorphism, may be due to several external factors. First, governments both influence and are influenced by large organizations in an institutional field. Assuming they act to their mutual benefit, large organizations and governments can and do influence formal and informal laws that govern all organizations in the institutional field.[49,50,51] This may take the form of political and financial support. Influence can also be subtle and indirect and often takes the form of trade associations and organized lobby groups. Educational organizations are also important in spreading isomorphism as accepted patterns of common behavior are reinforced through professional training. For example, possible mismanagement has been attributed by some observers to the prevalence of relatively short-term-oriented MBAs.[52,53]

Larger external economic, political, demographic and technological shocks can also impact institutional value systems positively and negatively. In addition, structural features such as an organization's relative age, size and position compared with other institutions are most important. Institutional theorists generally argue that larger and older organizations will resemble one another and follow one another's behavior.

Internal Factors

An organization's ability to manage and mismanage is directly related to the strength and independence of its own system of values or ideology. Most definitions of organizational ideology and culture can be reduced to some form of collective appreciative system involving the "shared" values and actions of its members that have accumulated over time.[54,55,56,57,58,59,60,61,62] Ideology is the worldview, or the shared ethical lens through which reality is experienced and understood by an organization. Its effectiveness hinges on appeals to logic and emotion.[63] Ideology is at times both beneficial and destructive. The institutional fortress concept suggests that ideology will converge to industry norms within a highly institutionalized context.

Conclusion

A recent comprehensive review of strategy concepts notes that management literature continues to devote significant attention to highly rationalized and prescriptive frameworks which focus on an organization's task and technical activities.[64] It is argued here that a deeper understanding of an organization's institutional environment, although until recently largely neglected, provides another valuable level of analysis.

This chapter pulls together streams of thought regarding "institutionalization" both within and around an organization. In order to explore and better understand the process of institutionalization, the major constructs available in the growing field of institutional theory were examined. The image of an institutional fortress is developed which provides a conceptual descriptive lens with which to view the nature and dynamics of the institutional walls that form around the key input and output activities of established organizations. The case of Canadian banks is offered as an example of strong isomorphism and institutionalization within an industry. Many countries have similar written laws and unwritten norms that combine to provide fortress-like protection for their financial services industry.

Isomorphic behavior is transmitted between organizations through written and unwritten norms, ideology and structural features such as an organization's relative age and size.

Contrary to prescriptive strategy explanations of services industry management, the institutional fortress model of mismanagement is offered as a first step in explaining why highly institutionalized financial service industry organizations are comprised of rational individuals who collectively at times "mismanage," or behave irrationally.

Chapter 4

Contrarian Risk Management and Fraud

Case 2: The Parmalat Fraud

Chapter Summary

This award-winning essay discusses the fraud surrounding Paramalat, an Italian cheese company.[1] The central idea is that investment bankers

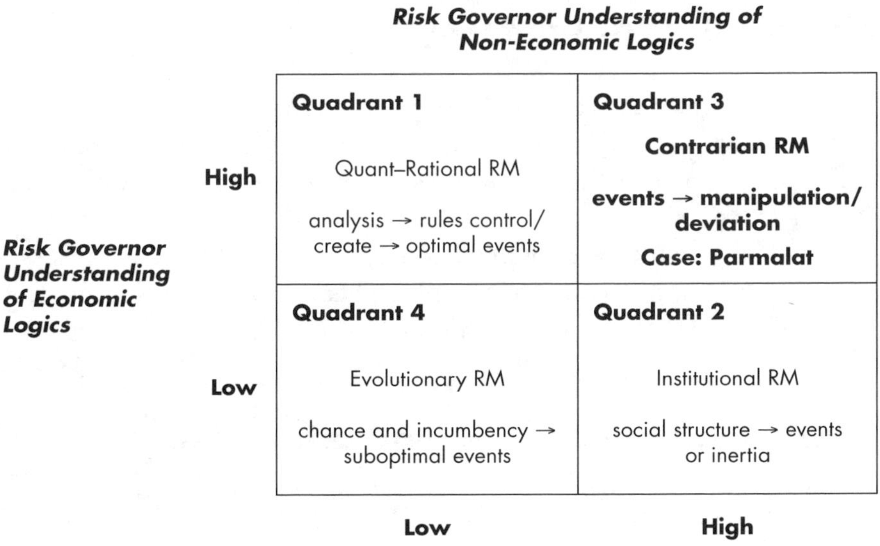

Risk Governor Understanding of Non-Economic Logics

	Quadrant 1	Quadrant 3
High	Quant–Rational RM analysis → rules control/ create → optimal events	**Contrarian RM** events → manipulation/ deviation **Case: Parmalat**
Low	**Quadrant 4** Evolutionary RM chance and incumbency → suboptimal events	**Quadrant 2** Institutional RM social structure → events or inertia

Risk Governor Understanding of Economic Logics

Low	High

FIGURE 4.1 The Holistic Risk Management Model (HRMM)

Source: Vit (1996)

were manipulated by fraudsters' knowledge of both rules and the social desirability of doing highly profitable foggy deals with the company. I call the manipulators "contrarians" and the investment banks that ran with the herd "conformists," and I discuss the multiple logics that were used in this fraud. An early version of the Holistic Risk Management Model (HRMM) is used to explain what happened.

Multiple Logics of Conformity and Contrarianism: The Problem with Investment Banks and Bankers

Brian: Look, you've got it all wrong! You don't need to follow me! You don't need to follow anybody! You've got to think for yourselves! You're all individuals!
Crowd: Yes, we're all individuals!
Brian: You're all different!
Crowd: Yes, we are all different![2]

The Problem of Conformity

Following on from the above observations of Terry Jones, the central idea of this chapter is that large organizations such as investment banks are full of clever people that often behave collectively in a silly fashion.[3] Why is this so?

I shall begin with an example of conformity that resulted in big losses for a group of large investment banks. Theory related to the multiple logics of conformity and contrarianism will then follow.

Paramalat: "Collective Madness of Banks"

On Friday December 19, 2003, Parmalat S.p.A. declared that a company bank account that was supposed to have a cash balance of close to $5 billion did not exist.[4] It explained that on December 17, 2003, Bank of America told one of Parmalat's auditors, Grant Thornton S.p.A., that a document confirming that a Parmalat finance entity in the Cayman Islands, Bonlat Financing Corp. (Bonlat), had a deposit of €3.95 billion ($4.9 billion) was false. On December 23, 2003, the company indicated that it could not account for additional funds and that a total of €7 billion ($8.7 billion) was unaccounted for. Parmalat filed for Italian bankruptcy protection on the same day. To date, Parmalat appears to have understated its liabilities by $11.7 billion, and an Italian investigation subsequently found numerous Parmalat employees guilty of fraud and sentenced them to jail terms.[5]

A closer examination of Parmalat's financial statements suggests that lending money to Parmalat did not make much economic sense, even if its false numbers were assumed to be sound. In particular, many warning signs that existed a priori were ignored.

For example, financial opaqueness was a major concern. It has also been noted that investment bank analysts repeatedly asked Parmalat why it continued with a large borrowing program when its balance sheet showed large cash balances. They also questioned why Parmalat used large and highly complex offshore financial structures and derivatives deals. For example, by 2002 Parmalat was investing in an unusual financing with Citigroup Inc. that effectively allowed Parmalat to borrow money from Citigroup that Parmalat categorized on its books as an investment. Citigroup moved the money through an entity called Buconero LLC, which means "black hole" in Italian. This seemed highly inappropriate for a dairy multinational corporation. Even though Parmalat was complex and operated approximately 135 plants and had 36,000 workers in 36 countries, it operated with more financial complexity than many of its peers.[6] Some suggest that the prospect of making large and immediate underwriting fees clouded the eco-logics of the investment banks' financial analysis.[7,8]

Investment banks decoupled from rational financial analysis.[9] They did not receive a satisfactory answer to an important question: why borrow and not use the billions of dollars of cash directly? This would cost less and make economic sense. For example, Dobson observed:

> However, more than a year before the meltdown at Parmalat one financial firm, Merrill Lynch, did report that it could not understand the need for Parmalat's opaque finances and advised investors to sell

shares in the firm . . . it is difficult to fathom why so many bankers and investors continued to lend to, or invest in, Parmalat until shortly before the firm's meltdown.[10]

In a report given to Italian prosecutors, Enrico Bondi, the special administrator appointed by the Italian government to restructure Parmalat, details where he believes some of the money went. Table 4.1 below shows that while acquisitions of $3.8 billion may have been usual for a large multinational corporation, its financial activity dwarfed its acquisition needs. Italy's central bank governor, Antonio Fazio, has said that although Parmalat's executives were clearly guilty of fraud on a large scale, its international investment bankers acted in a non-rational fashion. He called this "collective madness": "If there was an error or collective madness, it wasn't a collective madness of only the Italian banking sector."[11]

The balance of this chapter proposes a theory that endeavors to explain how economic rationality and learning are overridden by social

TABLE 4.1 Following the Money: Partial Accounting for Uses of Funds that Produced 14.2 Billion Euros of Debt for Parmalat

Items	Expenditure (billion euros)	Percent of total
Acquisitions	3.8	26.8%
Interest payments and fees related to bank debt	2.8	19.7%
Interest payments and fees related to bonds	2.5	17.6%
Siphoned off from the company	2.3	16.2%
Losses at operating units	1.6	11.3%
Taxes	0.9	6.3%
Dividends	0.3	2.1%
	TOTAL: 14.2	100.0%

Source: *Wall Street Journal* (2004) and Parmalat (2003)

forces. It is further assumed that some organizations can observe the collective appreciative systems and multiple logics of the organizational field of which they are a part, yet manage to learn from the non-learning of others to their advantage. I call these organizations "contrarian." For example, I contend that some banks did not participate in Parmalat risk because it did not make economic sense to them. Industry observers[12] have noted the following:

> Several large financial groups are conspicuous by their absence from the dozens of names embroiled in Parmalat's decline . . . Italy's Mediobanca did not lend the company a euro. Goldman Sachs did no advisory work. Lazard's relationship ended some time before Parmalat ran into trouble.

This deviance may be explained by mere chance. Vit, however, has suggested that non-conformity is not only related to contingency and incumbency, but that this phenomenon occurs intentionally and unintentionally at both the organizational field and organizational configuration levels of analysis.[13,14] For example, Vit explained how Australia's largest bank ignored multiple economic risk model warning signs over two years and eventually lost A$360 million in irregular currency options trading. In this case, it is ironic to note that the underlying economic logic of currency option pricing models, which incorporated the work of Nobel laureate Robert C. Merton (1973) among others, was overridden by social forces that can be explained by the ideas of his sociologist father, Robert K. Merton (1938).[15,16] Vit noted:

> NAB's board received a detailed presentation by its risk committee on lessons to be learned from the Allied Irish Bank trading losses. This briefing noted that frequent trading line excesses and audit exceptions were potential symptoms of a problem. Paradoxically, this was occurring at NAB in 2003, but was ignored and not questioned.[17]

This chapter looks at the special case of professional investment banking organizational fields and configurations and the relative convergence of non-learning over time.

Common Appreciative Systems Within Investment Banks

Recently, "institutionalists" have begun to explore multiple contrarian and conformist organizational logics within financial markets and insti-tutions.[18,19,20,21] A simple appreciative system framework is useful in exploring multiple logics at different levels of analysis. Figure 4.2 illustrates an appreciative system which is composed of packages of conformist-building mechanisms. Three groups of constructs, related to technical economic rationality (eco-logics), social cognitive routines (socio-logics) and normative predispositions (ideo-logics), create an appre-ciative system of powerful, mutually reinforcing forces of conformity.[22] This builds upon a framework anchored in the logics of economics and sociology proposed by Merton, Thompson and Tudon, and Vickers.[23,24,25]

Thus, the way organizations appreciate a situation collectively and individually results in conformist or deviant action that may threaten or ensure their survival.[26] Drawing from Vicker's and Simon's work, Figure 4.2 represents the appreciative system of investment banks both at a

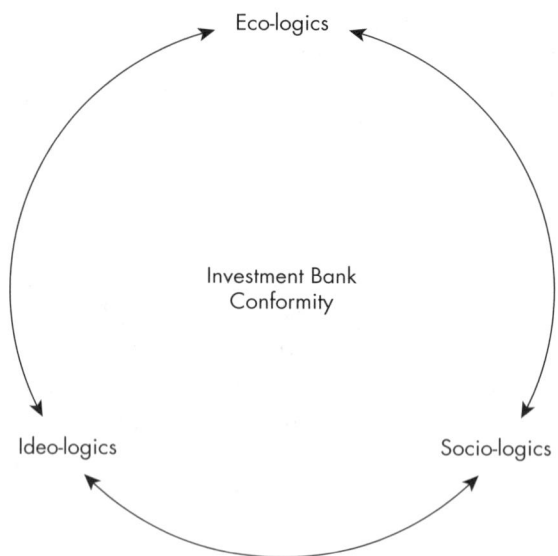

FIGURE 4.2 An Investment Banking Appreciative System

Source: Vit (2006)

collective organizational field level of analysis and also within individual bank configurations.[27,28]

The dominant Cartesian view of analysis would suggest that investment banks will predominantly rely upon eco-logics.[29] For example, the theory of investment analysis maps out this risk/return calculus in applied micro-economics.[30]

What is most interesting is the special case of when eco-logics do not make sense from the outset. This occurs when the collective players in an institutional field, such as investment banks, collectively ignore the underlying economic rationality of a situation over time.[31,32] Under conditions of uncertainty and complexity, conformist investment banks will select norms of rationality that will result in reliance upon common socio-logics and ideo-logics that override economic logic, sometimes with dramatic negative consequences.[33] Manipulative behavior may override intelligence. Parmalat appears to be such an example. In this case, it appears that the socio-logics and ideo-logics of investment banks partly overrode basic financial eco-logics.

For example, the discourses used to build legitimacy by investment banks, socio-logics and ideo-logics, are interesting to examine. Many terms, such as "risk arbitrage" exude confidence yet are relatively meaningless (arbitrage means to buy and simultaneously sell with no market risk). Worse, many investment banking terms mean the opposite of what they purport to mean. Phillips et al. (2004) have noted that discourse builds legitimacy and institutionalization.[34] Investment banking produces its own texts. For example, consider the term "investment" banking. The *Oxford Dictionary* defines "investment" as: "The conversion of money or circulating capital into some species of property from which an income or profit is expected to be derived in the ordinary course of trade or business."[35] It adds that this is:

> Distinguished from speculation, in which the object is the chance of reaping a rapid advantage by a sudden rise in the market price of something which is bought merely in order to be held until it can be thus advantageously sold again.[36]

Also, the term "hedge" common to finance, as in the term "hedge fund," is defined by the *Oxford Dictionary* to mean: "To secure oneself against loss on (a bet or other speculation) by making transactions on the other side so as to compensate more or less for possible loss on the first."[37]

Thus, Parmalat, and other recent financial meltdowns, demonstrate that taken-for-granted texts such as "investment" bankers engaging in "hedge-fund" investments are, in fact, institutionalized discourses and could be labeled differently (e.g. "speculators" engaging in "gambling") by those who step back from existing practice and create new understandings of social reality.

Institutional Theory: Organizational Field and Appreciative System Conformity

Institutional theorists define an organizational field as the totality of all relevant actors surrounding an organization.[38,39] In addition to being exposed to common technical economic models related to competition, institutional theorists suggest that an organization will face powerful social coercive, mimetic and normative institutionalizing mechanisms within an organizational field.[40] I call these eco-logics, socio-logics and ideo-logics respectively.[41] For example, large US banks have engaged in costly imitative behavior (LDC lending, real estate/thrift lending, telecom lending, Parmalat financing) and have reacted similarly to the coercive constraints of laws (money laundering legislation, disclosure, analysts' conflicts), regulations (geographic and product franchises) and deregulation (mega-mergers).

Adapted from a framework that sought to explain the breakdown of governance within a derivatives trading group, Figure 4.3 illustrates that organizations can be viewed on a continuum with respect to their collective reliance upon eco-logics, and socio- and ideo-logics.[42] On one end, organizations would have low reliance upon eco-logics. This means that quantitative financial models may not be fully understood or successfully applied. In this case, analysis may be socio-logics masquerading as eco-logics. Quadrant 2 in Figure 4.3 represents this state of nature.

On the other end, as represented by Quadrant 1, some organizations would fully rely upon and apply the dominant eco-logics within an organizational field. Furthermore, some outlier organizations may also have a high reliance upon eco-logics as well as socio- and ideo-logics.

Investment Bank Reliance upon
Socio-logics and Ideo-logics

	Quadrant 1	Quadrant 3
High	**1. Eco-logics Dominate** (Go by the book, no learning necessary)	**3. Contrarian** (Learn from 3 logics, deviate contrapuntally)
	Quadrant 4	Quadrant 2
Low	**Transient** (need to learn some or all logics)	**2. Socio-logics and/or Ideo-logics override** (decoupled, non-learning) E.g. Parmalat investment banks

Investment Bank
Reliance upon
Eco-logics

                    Low   **High**

FIGURE 4.3 Organizational Field Appreciative Systems: Investment Bank
Organizational Logics and Learning Implications

Source: Vit (2007)

Quadrant 3 of Figure 4.3 illustrates this case of "contrarian organizations" that appreciate the dynamics of the "herd" appreciative systems within the organizational field and selectively do not participate in bets due to their reliance on and understanding of the three logics. Finally, Quadrant 4 is a transient state whereby an organization does not rely on any of the three logics to coordinate its work. Apart from new organizations or those in deep crisis, it is unlikely that this state of nature would exist for long.[43]

Configuration Theory: Configurations and Appreciative System Conformity

Figure 4.3 highlighted one transient state of nature and three important cases. These constructs not only operate at a collective field level of analysis but also map on to an organizational level of analysis since configuration theory also suggests that a very similar system of forces will result in patterns of commonly observed organizational forms over time.[44] This also provides insight into conformist behavior. Building upon Thompson's (1967) coordinating mechanisms, Mintzberg proposes a conceptual system of organizational configurations, processes and standardization mechanisms.[45,46,47] These standardizing mechanisms can also be grouped together as eco-logics, socio-logics and ideo-logics that build organizational conformity. For example, standardization of work processes results in internal efficiency and may exist within a stable task environment.[48] Figure 4.4a below represents this case. Here, an organization relies upon eco-logics to coordinate its work. Large, older commercial banks within highly institutionalized industries are an example of these machine configurations. Learning for members of the operating core of these organizations is minimal since organizational routines have been developed by the organizations' techno-structure.[49,50]

Figure 4.4a suggests a low reliance upon external socio-logics and a high reliance upon dominant organizational eco-logics that may have evolved within a protected organizational field. For example, until recently, commercial banks in the United States were prohibited from

**Investment Bank Reliance upon
Socio-logics and Ideo-logics**

		Quadrant 1	Quadrant 3
	High	**1. Eco-logics Dominate**	**3. Contrarian**
Investment Bank Reliance upon Eco-logics		(Go by the book, no learning necessary)	(Learn from 3 logics, deviate contrapuntally)
		Quadrant 4	Quadrant 2
	Low	**Transient**	**2. Socio-logics and/or Ideo-logics override**
		(need to learn some or all logics)	(decoupled, non-learning)
			E.g. Parmalat investment banks
		Low	**High**

FIGURE 4.4a   Machine Configuration Pressures of Conformity (Quadrant 1 of Figure 4.3)

Source: Vit (2007)

engaging in investment banking activities such as the underwriting and sale of equities. This resulted in large product and geographic franchises which created machine bureaucracies that attempted to maximize efficiency. Thus, banking organizations that have a high reliance on eco-logics will have employees that will "go by the book" as the standardization of work processes and outputs is used to coordinate work within the configuration.

Similarly, the standardization of social skills and norms (socio-logics and ideo-logics) results in common behavior within investment banks. The professionalization and standardization of skills will allow for the accumulation of expert technical knowledge and "eco-logics" outside organizations that can be applied within organizations that wish to maximize proficiency. For example, equity analysts within the equity research department of an investment bank may largely rely upon their professional training (e.g. MBA, CFA, CPA) and this should lead to common approaches and conclusions regarding the financial viability and optimality of structures and clients, such as Parmalat.

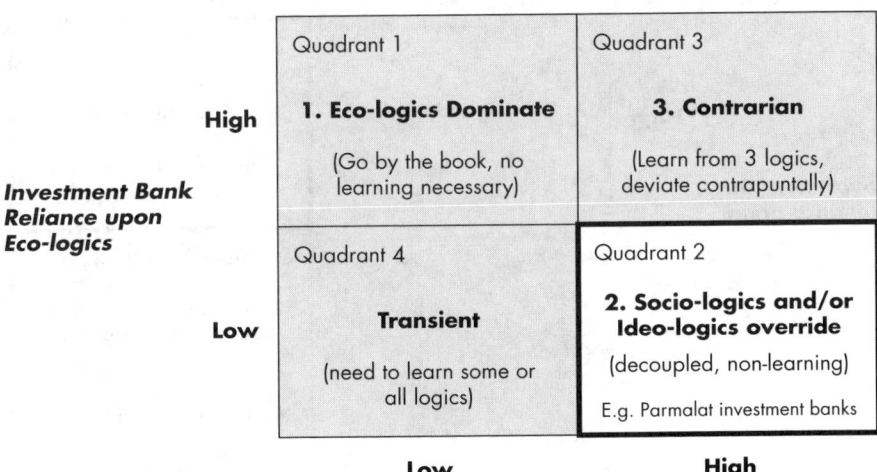

FIGURE 4.4b Professional Configuration Pressures of Conformity (Quadrant 2 of Figure 4.3)

Source: Vit (2007)

This rarely happens because professional socio-logics and social expertise are often also standardized outside yet reside within professional configurations such as investment banks. Related educational institutions, professional associations and financial markets reinforce common norms and discourses that become taken-for-granted and institutionalized.[51] Similar to the observations of older institutional theory, common professional norms will therefore eventually become nested and sedimentary within common professional configurations and reinforcing discourses and rhetoric that result in common strategy processes that override economic rationality.[52,53,54] Morison calls this social process limited identification. Figure 4.4b illustrates the phenomenon.[55]

Thus, contrarianism and conformity are also related to the standardizing forces that exist within configurations relative to the organizational field. For example, Abrahamson and Fairchild have called reliance upon eco-logics "real learning" and reliance upon socio-logics "superstitious learning," yet they suggest that non-retention of management fashions is under-explored.[56] Also, Staw and Epstein have noted that eco-logics

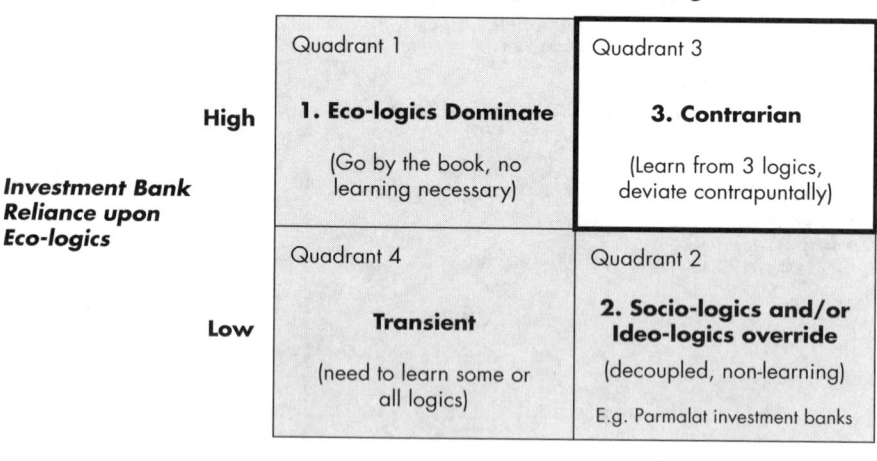

FIGURE 4.4c   Contrarian Learning from Pressures of Conformity (Quadrant 3 of Figure 4.3)

Source: Vit (2007)

related to modern management techniques do not systematically result in superior firm performance but do build socio-logics and legitimacy, and result in higher senior executive compensation.[57] I argue here that some contrarian configurations exist that do have the ability to observe these common appreciative systems.[58] Figure 4.4c illustrates that these organizations may be able to understand the three logics to their advantage, either intentionally or unintentionally.

This process is dynamic as a financial mania may involve infatuation with an industry sector financial bubble such as CLEC telecom companies, or smaller financial bubbles related to organizations such as Parmalat, over time.[59] At a higher level of analysis, it is therefore useful to enfold institutional and configuration theory with a dynamic theory of financial manias as discussed below.

Financial Mania Theory: Conformity within the Bubble Phase of a Financial Mania

Some financial theorists argue that each financial crisis is unique, temporarily destabilizing, and that market rationality and efficiency dominate. For the purposes of this chapter, I assume that the opposite is possible and agree with those that suggest that general conclusions can be made across time.[60,61] I will utilize the financial mania framework developed by Minsky (1972) and elaborated by Kindleberger.[62,63] Kindleberger's framework involves the four stages of displacement, boom/euphoria, mania/bubble and revulsion, which are briefly described below with regard to the role of bank credit.

Stage one begins with an exogenous event or outside shock to the system termed a "displacement." Kindleberger notes that this could take many forms, such as the adoption of an invention, a commodity glut, or the beginning or end of a war. Displacement introduces new opportunities for profits in some avenues and eliminates others. This concept is similar to the idea of discontinuities and disruptive technologies related to innovation.[64,65,66] Displacements may involve the introduction of not only new eco-logics but also new socio-logics to an organizational field. Thus, understanding how an organizational configuration responds to, and possibly learns from, a new displacement is important.

Stage two, the "boom" stage, begins when new opportunities overtake and dominate old ones. The involvement of investment bankers and the instability of bank credit are catalysts for the entire process. The easy availability of bank credit (and debt underwritten by investment bankers) at this stage fuels the boom. Over time, increased demand outstrips the capacity to supply goods or financial assets. Prices increase, creating new profit opportunities and speculation related to price increases. Near the end of stage two, "euphoria" kicks in as speculators begin betting upon price increases rather than on investment for production and sale. This is a term that Kindleberger notes Adam Smith called "overtrading." The danger of conformity is greater hereafter as mimetic herding by professional configurations may override the underlying science and potential of the displacement. This means that the override of eco-logics by socio-logics and ideo-logics by fluid market participants such as investment banks may be more possible as a mania evolves. Also, at this point contrarian organizations may be able to realize that transactions make social sense, but have stopped making economic sense.

Stage three, the "mania" or "bubble" stage, begins when exaggerated estimates of future cash flows come from euphoria and organizations or households see others making substantial gains from speculative trades. When the number of firms or individuals engaging in these transactions becomes large, Kindleberger argues that "speculation for profit leads away from normal rational behavior."[67]

Prices continue to increase until, at some stage, insiders decide to take their profits and exit, and market prices begin to stabilize as those exiting roughly match those entering. This leads to a period of financial distress as investment banks and others begin to realize markets will not go any higher. This concern finally leads to a stampede to get out of the market, panic selling for cash, and is sometimes precipitated by a shock such as a major bankruptcy or evidence of a swindle such as Parmalat. This results in the final stage, "revulsion." Revulsion leads financiers to stop financing any related activity entirely. This is then resolved by one of three mechanisms: prices fall so low that buyers for the assets again begin buying, trade limits are imposed or exchanges are closed, or a lender of last resort willing to grant credit emerges.

Enfolding Financial Mania Theory into Institutional and Configurational Logics

Figure 4.5 proposes a framework that suggests that a contrarian outlier may learn by means of a different appreciative system relative to its organizational field's rules and routines, and relative to its peers' common configurations.[68] In the special case of investment banks involved with large or small financial manias, contrarians may deviate significantly from the pack with favorable intended and unintended consequences by learning from the dynamics of the three logics of conformity. Contrarian organizations manage to maintain this contrarian social space over time. They do not join in the decoupling process as they understand tacitly or explicitly that economic logic no longer makes sense, and that social logics and ideologies are constructing sense.

Figure 4.5 concludes that less learning is possible for many conformist organizations in the third mania/bubble phase of a financial bubble as socio- and ideo-logics override economic rationality. Also, both

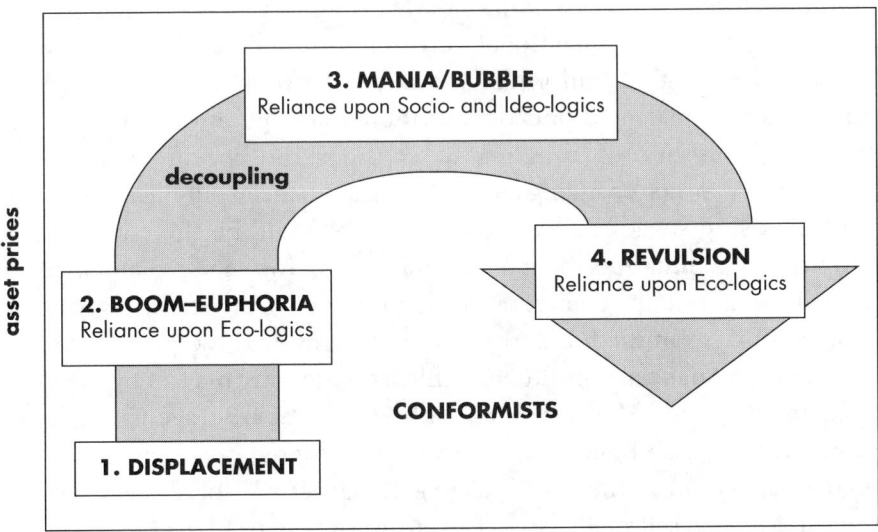

FIGURE 4.5 Logics in a Bubble

the boom and revulsion stages of a bubble rely on underlying rational micro-economic analysis and the execution of standardized rules and regulations.

Conclusion

This chapter contributes to the recent shift in research towards the study of multiple, competing organizational and institutional logics. It has presented a conceptual framework that connects the multiple logics underlying conformist and contrarian strategy with the boom–bust cycle of extreme institutionalization within capital markets. The framework explores common and unique deviations related to investment banking organizational fields and configurations, and their conformist and contrarian consequences for learning. An overall understanding of these processes has distinct and important consequences for the contrarian social distance produced. The mania related to expert investment bank analyst advice and financial institution risk taking in the case of Parmalat was used to further briefly illustrate these concepts.

The first implication of the framework developed here involves the role of learning from observing non-learning in an organizational field as a concept in organizational research. The theoretical framework presented highlights conformist and non-conformist tendencies at both the organizational field and organizational configuration levels. I have extended this line of thinking to consider the specific relationship between investment banking conformity and financial bubbles. An important next step suggested by the framework would be the comparative, empirical examination of financial mishaps across investment banking organizational fields, configurations and manias. For example, Abolafia and Kilduff examined the role of important market participants in containing a financial meltdown within a commodity market by means of enactment.[69] Also, Mello et al. have observed that arbitrageurs are sometimes aware of, and encourage, the taking of large positions by market participants prior to their collapse (e.g. Long-Term Capital Management, Enron, Metallgesellschaft) so as to take advantage of them.[70]

The broad relationships proposed here could serve as the beginning of the foundation for further analysis in terms of both selecting appropriate data and cases and in tracking and interpreting contrarian and conformist variance in results.

A second implication of this framework involves the issue of contrarianism. Non-institutionalization is treated here versus the evolution of institutionalization or deinstitutionalization.[71,72] Contrarian organizations understand determinism and endeavor to preserve agency both intentionally and emergently. Although contrarianism has been discussed as the antithesis of conformity, a more explicit treatment of contrarian processes could provide a useful basis for exploring contrarianism's temporal patterns. Consider the third "boom" stage of a financial market bubble. Further exploration of contrarian awareness, configuration and unique norms, and pseudo-contrarian non-awareness of mimetic and coercive institutional factors, together with an examination of key issues related to the tempo and constancy of such dynamics, could provide great utility in avoiding future costly herding behavior in financial markets and in other domains. For example, Lawrence et al. have noted not only that pace and stability of institutionalization over time may result in deinstitutionalization but also that other institutionalization trajectories are possible due to multiple forces.[73]

A third implication for research involves the role of structural conformity versus the role of agents who affect the contrarian strategy process. In this chapter, the focus on financial manias has led me to concentrate on conformist logics within investment banking organizational fields and configurations. Integrating the role of contrarian logics more fully would be worthwhile since contrarian configurations are the subjects and objects of agency. They understand, and deviate from, the institutional, configuration and financial mania conformist mechanisms described here.

A final important issue relates to management thinking itself. Contrarian theory is not simply the sum of unique unintended and intended consequences resulting from random deviation. Rather, contrarianism is a process that is related to different response mechanisms to observed conformist moves within organizational fields and configurations. Contrarian organizations find ways of resisting and maintaining distance that are shaped by unique appreciative systems, history and responses to intended and unintended mimetic and regulative moves and displacements within highly institutionalized organizational fields.

A fuller understanding of the contrarian learning process leads to a greater awareness of the need to maintain social distance and support contrary opinion. Management thinking and research should also resist conformist pressures and learn from non-learners, wherever or whoever they may be.

Chapter 5

Evolutionary Risk Management

Case 3: The National Australia Bank Fraud

Chapter Summary

This chapter examines how small events and routines were exploited by traders at National Australia Bank in order to defraud the bank. It uses

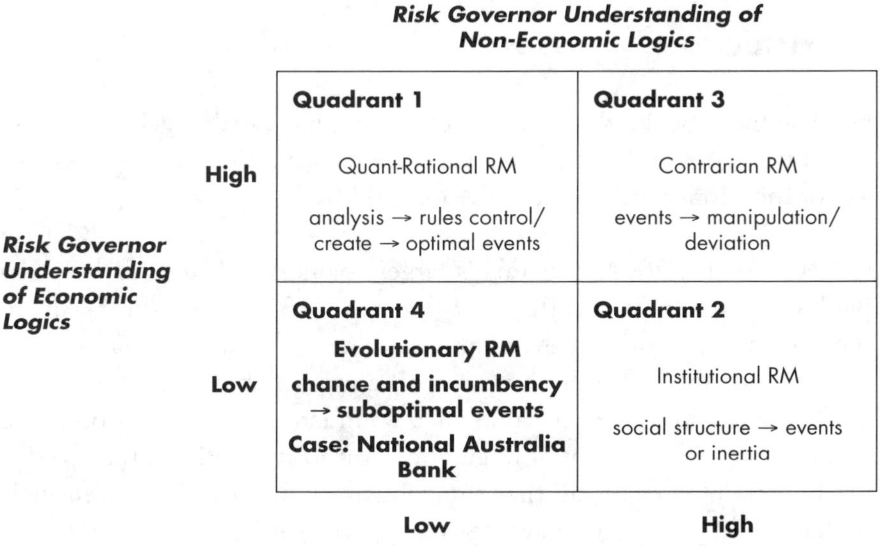

	Risk Governor Understanding of Non-Economic Logics	
	Quadrant 1	**Quadrant 3**
High	Quant-Rational RM analysis → rules control/ create → optimal events	Contrarian RM events → manipulation/ deviation
	Quadrant 4	**Quadrant 2**
Low	**Evolutionary RM** **chance and incumbency** **→ suboptimal events** **Case: National Australia** **Bank**	Institutional RM social structure → events or inertia
	Low	High

Risk Governor Understanding of Economic Logics (High / Low)

FIGURE 5.1 The Holistic Risk Management Model (HRMM)—Evolutionary Risk Management

an early version of the Holistic Risk Management Model (HRMM) framework that describes the interplay of economic and non-economic logics in creating organizational conformity and contrarianism. Data from a comprehensive report by the Australian Prudential Regulation Authority presented in 2004 is used to illustrate how the framework might be applied to explain the breakdown in risk management systems within Australia's largest bank, the National Australia Bank.

The framework presented helps to explain the decoupling of technical rationality by examining and illustrating cognitive and normative mechanisms that build legitimacy and reduce uncertainty. This leads to an illusory sense of control that can threaten the survival of an organization. An awareness of the different logics facing risk governors and risk takers within a large organization is another step towards understanding and possibly avoiding financial fraud. The chapter is original because it links a recent real world management meltdown with a conceptual framework that examines the social risk of risk management systems and the dialogue between organizational conformity and contrarianism. The illustrative data presented is also rare, since the subject organization has exceptionally made a confidential document public.

Introduction

> The fraud begins with a controlling fact, inescapably evident but all but universally ignored. It is that the future economic performance of the economy . . . cannot be foretold.[1]

On January 13, 2004, Australia's largest bank, the National Australia Bank (NAB), announced that it had lost Au$185 million due to unauthorized trading in currency options. The amount lost was revised upwards to Au$360 million in a NAB announcement on January 27, 2004. On March 23, 2004, a detailed confidential report was prepared by the Australian Prudential Regulation Authority (APRA). It arrived at the interesting conclusion that the collusive behavior of four renegade traders could and should have been stopped, as it had been consistently detected and reported by the bank's risk management systems. In particular, throughout 2003, every layer of NAB's risk management system received multiple warnings of highly irregular trading, yet all of these alarm bells were ignored. This included line management; back office; front office; risk committees; internal audit; and the principal board and its sub-committees. APRA concluded that the events were entirely avoidable: "On paper, NAB's existing control framework— despite its weaknesses—should have been able to identify and contain the risk positions of the traders."[2]

In order to provide transparency, on March 24, 2004, the National Australia Bank decided to make the confidential APRA report available to the public. The National's Chairman, Graham Kraehe, noted: "We fully accept APRA comments about the need for the Board to take a leadership role in transforming the culture and governance processes at the National."[3] This chapter draws on the data presented in the comprehensive APRA report, which includes references to available paper and electronic documents, a detailed report by the external auditors, and detailed interviews with numerous bank employees.

Despite the importance of understanding deviant and conformist pressures within an organization for advancing theories of management, and for practitioners of corporate governance within financial service organizations, few attempts have been made to link the real world micro-processes of risk management meltdowns with a conceptual framework. This chapter offers such a conceptual lens and is rooted in the logics of economics and sociology developed by Thompson and Tudon.[4]

The central idea of this framework, represented broadly in Figure 5.2, is that effective governance and risk management judgment as well as deception (organizational contrarianism) require an understanding of the dialogue between three management logics I call eco-logics, socio-logics and ideo-logics. These three logics and their interrelatedness are described below.

The Eco-logical View

Underlying an economics-based view of risk management systems is the assumption that individuals and groups within organizations make rational and unique choices. Applied micro-economics, or finance,

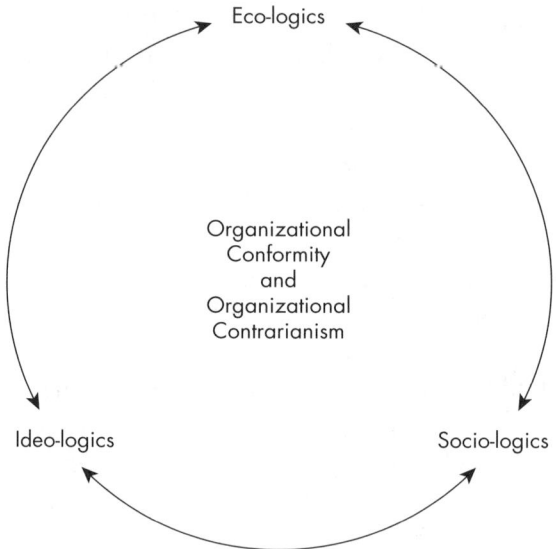

FIGURE 5.2 An Organizational Appreciative System

Source: Vit (2006)

is based upon the assumption that managers maximize returns while minimizing risks according to rational theories of choice and neoclassical economic theory.[5] Although classical "scientific management" approaches to managing are, at times, challenged as to their economic meaningfulness, most risk management systems assume that there is a logical and objective "best practice" that can quantify, optimize, manage and control risk. I call such approaches "eco-logics."

In the case of NAB, market risk control systems existed that were thought to be foolproof. These included two models that quantified trading limits and maximum possible losses to trading books (VaR and Greek letter methodologies). APRA concluded that at least one of the risk measurement models functioned properly, but was ignored by the traders' immediate superiors:

> While there was dispute regarding the accuracy of the value at risk (VaR) results, the undisputed "Greek" risk measures (delta, gamma, vega and theta) were also routinely exceeded. This demonstrates very poor limit discipline by the front office and its management.

Despite the currency market desk being in excess of limits almost daily, there was no serious effort by Global Markets to either bring the business back within mandated risk parameters, or undertake any rigorous reassessment of the adequacy of the existing limit structures.[6]

Using an open system of input, process and output,[7] Figure 5.3 outlines several of the major players in the NAB irregular trading affair. According to the eco-logical model, market risk information (inputs) regarding irregular trading activity should flow freely to those governing the organization (control process) and corrective action should be taken (output). The APRA report notes that each of the inputs noted in Figure 5.3 either failed to reach the appropriate governors of the organization or, when it did so, was ignored and no corrective action was taken.

APRA suggested that the eco-logics of NAB's risk management models worked, but the implementation of the model failed. For example, APRA concluded its NAB report by recommending that the appropriate inputs and channels of information be improved and that appropriate and "independent" risk managers use the models correctly. This assumes a rational formulation–implementation–control management model anchored in eco-logics.[8,9]

The Socio-logical View

According to the socio-logical view, the reason for the failure of NAB's rational market risk models may have less to do with the underlying

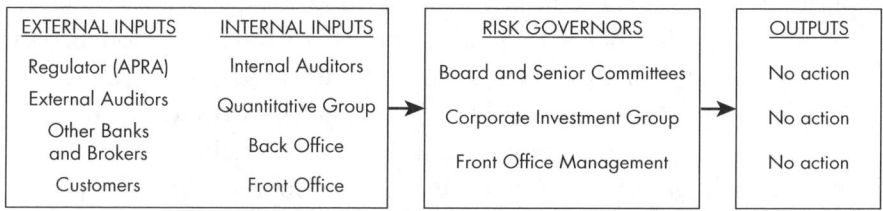

FIGURE 5.3 Eco-logics and Risk Management Inaction at NAB

Source: Vit (2006)

science of the models and their algorithms, and more to do with the social process of how the model's facts were selected, valued and acted upon.[10,11] Large and older bureaucracies such as banks often have a worldview of risk taking that reinforces conformist behavior which at times can lead to mismanagement.[12] Institutional theory suggests that organizations cannot be very different primarily due to social reasons I call socio-logics. Over time, organizations, and the totality of relevant actors within them, will begin to look and act alike. For example, DiMaggio and Powell observe that while "competitive isomorphism" looks at conformist forces in economic terms within freely competitive markets (eco-logics), it does not adequately explain conformist behavior. Instead, they focus upon non-economic social processes that build and maintain conformity, which they call "institutional isomorphism."[13]

Institutional theorists also suggest that large bureaucratic organizations are institutions within which very powerful social forces exist that encourage conformity.[14] Two general social sources of conformity are coercive reasons such as laws and rules (often measured by eco-logics) and imitative reasons such as herding behavior within financial markets and organizations.[15] Experienced managers also rely upon embedded cognitive routines that recognize and imitate reliable patterns for success.[16] Thus, the socio-logics of rules, routines and ceremonies co-ordinate work and promote efficiency within large machine bureaucracies.[17,18,19,20,21] In the special case of risk management, socio-logics can sometimes eclipse eco-logics and lead to an illusion of control.

For example, within a large commercial bank, a socio-logic might dictate that in the highly complex mathematical world of currency options trading, in order to reduce uncertainty and build legitimacy, risk governors (see Figure 5.1) may not question the eco-logics and scientific application of the models. In fact, whether or not the black boxes work may become irrelevant, as they are decoupled from the rationality of the technical core of the risk systems, and are used purely for sociological and ceremonial purposes.[22,23,24] For example, irrespective of their understanding of whether or not wealth is being created, the senior management of a large bank may not feel it is an important industry player unless it too has an exotic currency options trading desk.

In the case of NAB, APRA has explained that the original economic and strategic rationale of setting up the currency options trading desk was to serve corporate clients. Yet, throughout 2003 a decoupling of these eco-logics took place as large market risk bets were taken by the currency options trading desk for its own account, with other banks. APRA again notes this decoupling of eco-logics by front office management:

> The business strategy of Global Markets was to increase revenue from sales of financial products to customers and to reduce trading revenue as a percentage of total revenue . . . The desk had actual option exposures that were heavily concentrated amongst a few interbank counterparties . . . Given that this desk profile was out of line with CIB's business strategy and the knowledge that the desk continually exceeded risk limits, it is clear that Global Markets management oversight of the desk was inadequate.[25]

NAB's currency options group incurred heavy losses when its bets did not pan out, particularly after betting that the US dollar would appreciate in September 2003 after a G7 meeting when it in fact did the opposite. This resulted in large losses which, along with other smaller losses, necessitated their concealment by means of the creation of fictive trades and accounts. As explained above, even though four currency options traders tampered with the risk management eco-logics at NAB, the technology that monitored market risk excesses did send alarm bells to the internal and external parties highlighted in Figure 5.3. In almost every case institutional, not technical economic, reasons inhibited action.

For example, APRA notes that the bank's internal auditors were very concerned about limit excesses and endeavored to escalate their concern to senior management throughout 2003. At the same time, however, the mechanism for escalating concerns was changed from a rating scale of 1 to 6 to a scale of 1 to 3, so that fewer items were raised for senior management attention. A similar socio-logic, whether intended or unintended, is observed by Chomsky, who suggests that one method of limiting critical questioning is to create a social structure that does not allow sufficient time or social space for problems to be framed or addressed, a limiting process he calls the genius of concision.[26]

Also, APRA, the national bank supervising body, expressed its concerns about improper currency trading in January 2003 in a letter to NAB's senior management. Yet, APRA's concerns were ignored by

NAB's senior management until one year later, when an employee's incessant concerns finally flagged the irregular trading. Furthermore, the APRA report underlined that NAB's external auditors, KPMG, identified 800 limit breaches and lack of reporting related to the currency options desk in an important letter addressed to NAB Finance Management on December 10, 2003.

A third source of conformity is cultural or normative. The standardization of common norms and values is sometimes broadly referred to as ideology.[27,28] It is a normative conformist mechanism that is underpinned by deep and invisible values within an organization that I call the organization's ideo-logic.

The Ideo-logical View

The eco-logical view of risk management looks at the technical efficiency of products, systems and markets. It assumes certainty and rationality. The socio-logical view of risk systems looks at what happens when rationality is decoupled and external legitimacy-building behavior overrides rationality. This is a cognitive process that relies on the embedding of reassuring routines and the common actions of others to make sense of complex and volatile environments.[29]

The ideo-logical view of risk management is different from these two views. It looks at the shared feeling of belonging of the members of an organization so they identify with it that may mobilize members to make efforts on behalf of the group, or internalize its values.[30,31] Older organizations are infused with deeply rooted common shared values or "culture." This is often originated by their founders.[32,33] Some organizations, such as missionary organizations, principally coordinate human behavior by the standardization of norms that I call ideo-logics.[34] Westley and Bird observed that ideology is most powerful in the hands of leaders who appeal to both reason and emotion.[35] Thus, ideo-logics are the shared ethical lenses that determine how facts are selected, valued and acted (or not acted) upon. Similar to the auto-pilot system of an aircraft, the ideo-logics of a group act as a regulator that will use the eco-logics and socio-logics of an organization advantageously for the benefit of the greater good of the entire organization. When the three logics of a group and those of a larger machine bureaucracy are mutually reinforcing, this is advantageous to the organization. I call this organizational conformity.

Yet, group definitions within organizations can be fuzzy and complex.[36] Sub-groups sometimes identify more strongly with themselves (in-group) than with other groups (out-groups) within an organization. Cultural cleavages exist between different groups in an organization that may override an organization's overall dominant norms. Sub-groups may use eco-logics and socio-logics to advance norms related to self-interest. I call this process organizational contrarianism.

For example, executive compensation is often highly correlated with short-term financial results of sub-groups, which may conflict with the long-term financial viability of a financial services organization. Thus, the underlying short-term performance norms of sub-groups that are traders and sub-groups that are their supervisors may create the incentive to make sizable profits and to ask few questions. Galbraith calls this the economics of innocent fraud.[37]

In the case of NAB, the APRA report, although mainly concerned with righting the eco-logic of NAB, underlines the overall culture at NAB as one of the biggest contributors to the options trading losses. APRA distinguishes between the culture of the trading desk and that of NAB overall.[38] It noted that there was a lack of separation of risk managers and business managers, and an inability to escalate concerns to senior officers within the organization:

> By the term "culture" we refer not only to the working environment within the dealing room and the personal attitudes and behaviors of individuals associated with the currency options desk, but also to the wider environment within the bank and the attitudes displayed by key decision makers to principles of risk management, transparency and candor . . . In this section two clear themes emerge: the profit motive, or performance culture, and its skewing of the "business partnership" balance between risk management and business decision making; and, a close management of information flows that discourages the escalation of issues of concern to the board or to relevant external parties (such as APRA).

David Bullen, the renegade trader who was at the center of the irregular trading, summarized this decoupling as follows:

In my experience at the bank I had had no contact with any management above the level of the currency options desk head. I had never met Sam's boss, for example, and there seemed to be a "leave it alone" attitude as long as all seemed well. This was a little ludicrous, with all the managers up the tree happy to believe what was told to them from the level below. Management at higher levels seemed preoccupied with running the business and took little interest in what was going on below them unless they were forced to get involved . . . Tell the people what they want to hear, and no one will rock the boat. Give no one reason to doubt, and they will look no further.[39]

Organizational Conformity and Contrarianism: An Appreciative System of Eco-logics, Socio-logics and Ideo-logics

An important question within large machine bureaucracies such as established financial services organizations is: to what extent can the governors responsible for risk management within these organizations understand the multiple logics at work within an organization and act independently? I have outlined the three logics that have all tried to deal with this question and the dialogue between organizational conformity and contrarianism.

Although the standardization of work processes and outputs (eco-logics) appears to be most dominant within a bureaucracy, the standardization of skills (eco- and socio-logics) and norms (ideo-logics) is required to achieve further coordination within an organization. This also reinforces conformity. The paradox of organizational conformity is that it requires a deep understanding of the technical eco-logics of management systems (such as market risk models), as well as the socio-logics of cognitive templates and normative ideo-logics used by sub-groups and the organization overall.

Effective management requires a certain awareness and critical questioning of deviant behavior within the organization. For example, this means that the eco-logics, socio-logics and ideo-logics of risk governors and risk takers within a bank's risk management system should be mutually reinforcing and promote the identification and escalation of irregular financial activity. The broad distinction made in this chapter is that the degree to which a governing group can exercise independent risk judgment is related to its ability to first appreciate and then limit significant deviation in risk processes at the eco-logical, socio-logical and ideo-logical angles of analysis.

Contrarian and Conformist Appreciative Systems and Risk

The multiple perspectives used to track excessive risk discussed above, eco-logics,[40] socio-logics[41] and ideo-logics,[42] are artificially separated for analytic purposes. They represent a more complex interaction, as norms are nested within social pressures, which in turn are pressured by norms, which both form intended eco-logics and unintended outcomes.[43,44,45] Vickers builds upon Simon's (1945) work and suggests that judgment (and lack of judgment) are linked to an understanding of the cognitive and normative predisposition of individuals, organizations and society to select, value and act upon facts. He calls this an appreciative system and notes:[46,47]

> Appreciation manifests itself in the exercise through time of mutually related judgments of reality and value. These appreciative judgments reflect the view currently held by those who make them of their interests and responsibilities, views largely implicit and unconscious which none the less condition what events and relations they will regard as relevant or possibly relevant to them . . . Such judgments disclose what can best be described as a set of readinesses to distinguish some aspects of the situation rather than others and to classify and value these in this way rather than in that. I will describe these readinesses as an appreciative system.[48]

Merton calls compliance with social structures and mechanisms related to cultural goals (ends) and institutional norms (means) conformity, and non-compliance with both rebellion. I call consistency in the outcomes of this appreciative process, or the formation and maintenance of a common pattern in the actions of actors in an organization operating under these three logics, organizational conformity.

Figure 5.4 summarizes the three logics that form a risk appreciative system and illustrates them using the recent case of regular irregular currency options trading at NAB. The risk appreciative system presented in Figure 5.4 represents all three logics, or three sets of micro-processes. They are eco-logics, socio-logics and ideo-logics. The framework can be viewed from two vantage points, those of risk conformers and risk contrarians. Effective risk governance requires a deep understanding of the three logics and independence of thought and action in detecting deviations in any of the logics that could result in abuse. The contrarian

	Eco-logics	**Socio-logics**	**Ideo-logics**
Coordinating Mechanisms	Standardization of Work Processes and Outputs	Standardization of Skills	Standardization of Norms
Conformist Mechanisms	– rational rules – economic models – algorithms – quantitative methods	– values, norms – identification – internalization – loyalty	– values, norms – identification – internalization – loyalty
Contrarian Deviation in Mechanisms	– technology tampering	– exploiting rules – reinforcing ceremony	– cultural cleavage – in-group vs. out-group
National Australia Bank			
	Eco-logics	**Socio-logics**	**Ideo-logics**
Conformist Mechanisms	– VaR methodology – Greek letter report – internal compliance systems – corporate customer focus strategy	– lack of audit independence – lack of escalation procedures – symbols of legitimacy – options trading money machine	– profit is king – illusion of control – no need to escalate
Contrarian Deviation in Mechanisms	– technology tampering – trade cancellations – fictive trades and reporting – inter-bank/proprietary trading strategy	– interbank trading, not corporate trading – approvals obtained for excesses – black box broken	– profit is king – avoid escalation – limited identification – trader cults

FIGURE 5.4 A Risk Management Appreciative System Application: NAB

Source: Vit (2006)

utilizes precisely the same calculus and exploits deviations in some or all of the three logics.

Figure 5.4 illustrates, for example, that NAB's rogue traders were able to manipulate the three logics to their advantage. First, they successfully argued that the bank's eco-logics were incorrect (the VaR model does not work properly) and physically attempted to alter and disguise some of the parameters of permissible trading limits and losses using NAB's computer systems. Socio-logics reinforced this aberrant behavior as the routines of constant profits and the complexity of the eco-logics resulted in a decoupling of meaningful risk monitoring and control. Ceremony and legitimacy building overrode the economic fact that many reports were showing irregular trading activity. In addition, a self-serving trading room ethos, or ideo-logic, prevented any meaningful escalation of multiple warning signs. Also, according to APRA, a NAB-wide ideo-logic existed that prevented the escalation of concerns and confounded business management with risk management.

Effective governance requires the alignment of low deviation of all three logics. This requires an understanding and independent questioning of all three logics. For example, NAB's board received a detailed presentation by its risk committee on lessons to be learned from the Allied Irish Bank trading losses. This briefing noted that frequent trading line excesses and audit exceptions were potential symptoms of a problem. Paradoxically, this was occurring at NAB in 2003, but was ignored and not questioned.

The framework of organizational conformity and contrarianism put forward here rests on several fundamental assumptions. Contrarianism will occur when a unique appreciative system exists that resists common logics within an organization. This unique system creates and maintains social contrarian distance by explicitly or implicitly understanding how organizational conformity is maintained. This contrarian distance results in unique intended and unique unintended consequences or organizational contrarianism.[49,50] At the same time, effective organizational risk governance requires similar understanding of these three levels of analysis and an appreciative system of social regulation that closes this contrarian gap.

Implications for Governance Theorists and Practitioners

The paradox underscored by this chapter is that effective organizational conformity requires an awareness of the possibilities of organizational contrarianism. Conversely, effective organizational contrarianism may result from an awareness of the logics and the mechanisms within them that promote organizational conformity.

Contrarianism occurs when several factors that promote and maintain contrarian distance exist. Several preliminary ideas that may be considered for further practical confirmation and future research are offered below to explain this process.

Contrarian groups may remain marginal due to their age, size or perspective. Mintzberg suggests that smaller and younger organizations may have different ideologies due to their entrepreneurial founders.[51] Thus, newer innovative configurations that are predominantly driven by ideo-logics to break rules may be nested within older configurations that are co-ordinated by eco-logics that maximize efficiency. Socio-logics act as a countervailing force and catalyst that decouples eco-logics, and may allow contrarian groups to engage in deviant action based upon their different ideo-logics.

Contrarianism is not simply acting differently or looking different. It is a unique ideo-logic-based process nested within larger socio-logical and eco-logical processes. Due to their unique appreciative system and configuration, contrarian groups are aware of the divergence of strategic ideas, configurations and action. Thus, contrarian groups must be insular enough to tolerate error and uncertainty and exploit the logics of conformity. This tolerance for uncertainty, ambiguity and error is reflected more formally by a unique system of values and group configuration relative to its peers.[52,53,54,55]

A further implication of contrarianism is that risk governors must also understand these dynamics in order to maintain organizational conformity. Lack of understanding of the three logics may result in organizations that adopt so-called innovative practices when, in fact, risk governors may be engaged in mimetic conformist behavior that could threaten their survival.

These constructs are offered as a first step in understanding contrarian and conformist processes. In the context of bureaucracies that must control large risks, the challenge, then, is to create theory to understand conformity and contrarianism. This chapter is an initial contribution to creating a conceptual treatment of risk management using multiple logics within the context of a case study of a recent risk management breakdown. It is of relevance to management theorists and practitioners as it contributes to our understanding of the risk in risk management systems.

Chapter 6

Evolutionary Risk Management

Case 4: The Gaspesia Project Fiasco

Chapter Summary

The Gaspesia case study examines the non-economic conformity of governments, unions and firms that engaged in a large project failure within a competitive industry. Although the principal actors in this event

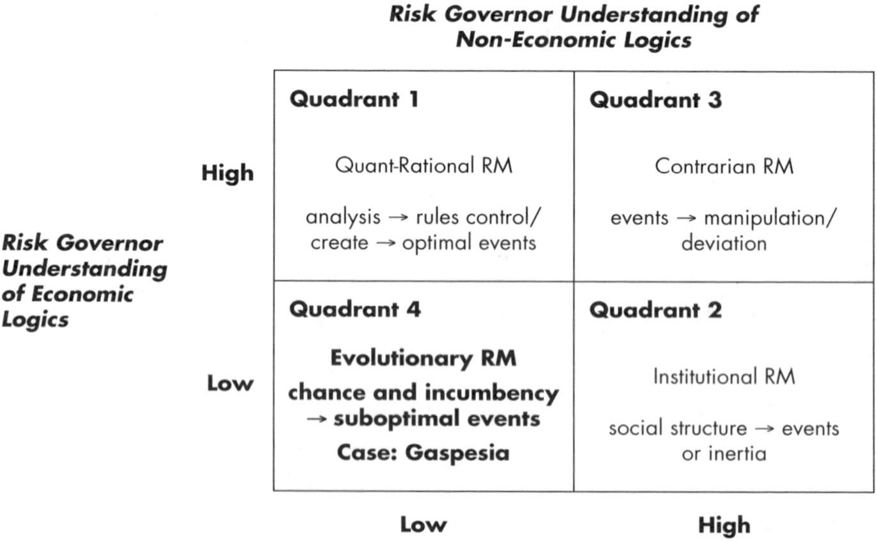

Risk Governor Understanding of Non-Economic Logics

		Quadrant 1	**Quadrant 3**
	High	Quant-Rational RM analysis → rules control/ create → optimal events	Contrarian RM events → manipulation/ deviation
Risk Governor Understanding of Economic Logics		**Quadrant 4**	**Quadrant 2**
	Low	**Evolutionary RM** **chance and incumbency** **→ suboptimal events** **Case: Gaspesia**	Institutional RM social structure → events or inertia
		Low	**High**

FIGURE 6.1 The Holistic Risk Management Model (HRMM)—Evolutionary Risk Management

ostensibly responded to economic rationality, social and normative pressures overrode the market rationality of government institutions, firms, communities and investors. The HRMM's evolutionary risk management mode of operating is exemplified by Tembec, the notional project manager, which was buffeted by chance events and the routines of the governments and unions involved.

This chapter will trace the evolution and failure of this large project. It argues that institutional and organizational processes help explain why some organizations respond to bad news by continually ignoring it. This inside view is a process that has been called conformist strategy.[1]

Justice Robert Lesage's public inquiry concluded that the $325 million losses incurred by Gaspesia project investors were mainly due to non-economic reasons.[2] A loss of such magnitude is a rare event and merits closer scrutiny. The study also presents a version of the Holistic Risk Management Model that explains that this is due to reliance upon confounded and different economic, ideological and social logics by different actors. When there is inconsistent and low understanding of these logics, small chance events and routines add up to big problems. This is the passive state within the HRMM called evolutionary risk management.

The Gaspesia Project Failure

On December 17, 2001, the premier of Quebec, Bernard Landry, announced plans for the reopening of a paper mill in Chandler, Gaspe, Canada. The project was expected to create 260 jobs. The estimated cost was $465 million, the majority of which would be financed by public funds, with a $35 million investment by a private sector operator, Tembec Inc. The mill never operated, and the project was abandoned on January 30, 2004, with construction having been 40.7 percent completed. Successive cost overruns had driven its projected final cost to over $700 million. The partnership, Papiers Gaspesia Inc., filed for protection from creditors under Canadian law on February 10, 2004. An appreciative system framework comprising economic, social and ideological logics will be used in order to determine why, and how, this happened.

Prior Research on Project Escalation of Commitment

Why are projects that are clearly economic failures allowed to live for long periods at great cost? Previous escalation of commitment research has sought answers to this question. Staw conducted three experimental studies and suggested that there is a dialogue between three sets of constructs.[3] First, the past decisions of individuals can be used to justify new actions retrospectively due to internal and external needs to demonstrate competence. Also, cultural and organizational pressures for consistency may increase commitment. Finally and prospectively, the perceived probability and value of future outcomes build commitment to a course of action. Ross and Staw build upon this work and used a case study to demonstrate that organizational persistence escalated the costs of a nuclear power plant from $75 million to $5 billion over 23 years.[4] They concluded that there were five main categories of causes that resulted in the escalation of commitment to projects. These determinants were related to project, psychological, social, organizational and contextual factors. Keil observes that project escalation in software projects is due to similar reasons.[5] He prescribes early and frequent risk assessment, independent audits throughout different stages of a project by different groups, and the separation of initial and subsequent decision-makers and decisions via manager rotation, which avoids the need for self-justification by committed project founders. The effects of prescriptions, however, are not obvious within complex systems. For example, McNamara et al. suggest that increased banker monitoring was partly beneficial, but also actually produced unintended negative consequences.[6] Projects often involve multiple stakeholders and sub-cultures. Golden-Biddle and Rao observe that the identity of boards with multiple stakeholders is not monolithic and that hybrid identities increase intra-organizational conflict and confusion.[7] Miller et al. note that simplicity, or managers' perceptions and overconfidence in their own efficacy that narrows down their field of vision and so excludes other possibilities, may contribute to organizational inertia and commitment.[8] Conversely, Ocasio argues that strategic attention and focus can be beneficial if organizational decision-makers concentrate on a small number of possibilities.[9] He proposes an attention-based view of the firm that combines the focus, situation and structural distribution of attention which is similar to the aforementioned drivers of Ross and Staw.[10]

Similarly, in their study of six grand-scale projects, Shapira and Berndt (1997) developed several propositions and conclusions.[11] They proposed that even though objective data suggests that a project does not make economic sense, promoters believe that their odds of success are very good. They call this narrow framing. Also, when promoting a project, the project champions present the project as a special case and reject all evidence related to comparable projects as incomparable. They call this closure an inside view which creates scenario thinking that shuts out data on similar unsuccessful projects and emphasizes an extreme subjective view. In the construction phase, Shapira and Berndt suggest that two routes are open to project champions when they realize their project is failing.[12] They distinguish between two focuses, survival and aspiration. If survival is at risk, risk takers face extinction and will be risk averse. If survival is not at risk, project participants will focus on a second route, that of achieving an aspiration level that defines success. Great risks can be taken in this case as there is no downside. This was the case for all of the participants in the Gaspesia project discussed below. The survival of the project partners was never on the line. Thus, attention turned to achieving their aspirations and the highly risky behavior of making the project happen.

Institutional theory also examines multiple normative, social and economic constructs that exist within project escalation of commitment theory. Institutional theorists note that normative predispositions and tacit values on the part of organizations create powerful subjective schemas of understanding that greatly influence outcomes. I broadly call these ideo-logics. Institutionalists have also highlighted how interrelated legitimacy-building forces, related to coercive and mimetic mechanisms within government agencies, unions and firms in an organizational field, divorce themselves from economic sense. I call these forces socio-logics. Together with underlying technical and economic rationality that I call eco-logics, these three logics combine to form internal reinforcing frames, or appreciative systems, as illustrated in Figure 6.2. It is adapted from a framework proposed by Vit.[13,14]

This chapter describes how different project participants relied upon different logics in understanding and misunderstanding the Gaspesia

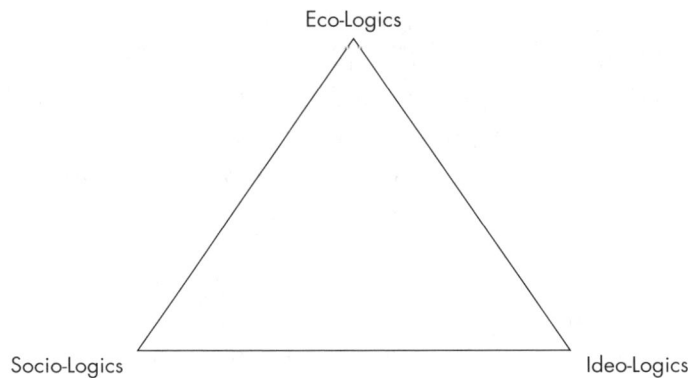

FIGURE 6.2 Gaspesia Project Actor Appreciative System

Source: Vit (2010)

project. This resulted in four different strategy processes that help illuminate why the Gaspesia project failed. They are represented as rational, evolutionary, institutional and judicious risk management in Figure 6.3.

A second and parallel body of knowledge that provides further utility in understanding appreciative systems and closure is organizational configuration theory. This case study will demonstrate that powerful organization-level conformist processes resulted in the standardization of norms, cognitive routines and decision rules within government lending agencies and unions. It will describe how these formed different appreciative systems or schemas in a failed project that eclipsed economic viability (Quadrant 1) and resulted in institutional risk management (Quadrant 2).[15] This chapter will also demonstrate that a complete lack of understanding related to all three logics, evolutionary risk management (Quadrant 4), existed on the part of its notional project leader. Last, this chapter proposes that judicious risk management (Quadrant 3) involves the ability to understand and rely upon multiple logics.

It is curious to note that the Gaspesia project failure demonstrates that although the project showed no economic and technical feasibility throughout its pre-construction and construction phases (Quadrant 1), project champions relied upon powerful socio-logics and ideo-logics to shut down these eco-logics (Quadrant 2). Furthermore, the notional project leader's lack of understanding of these logics created space for

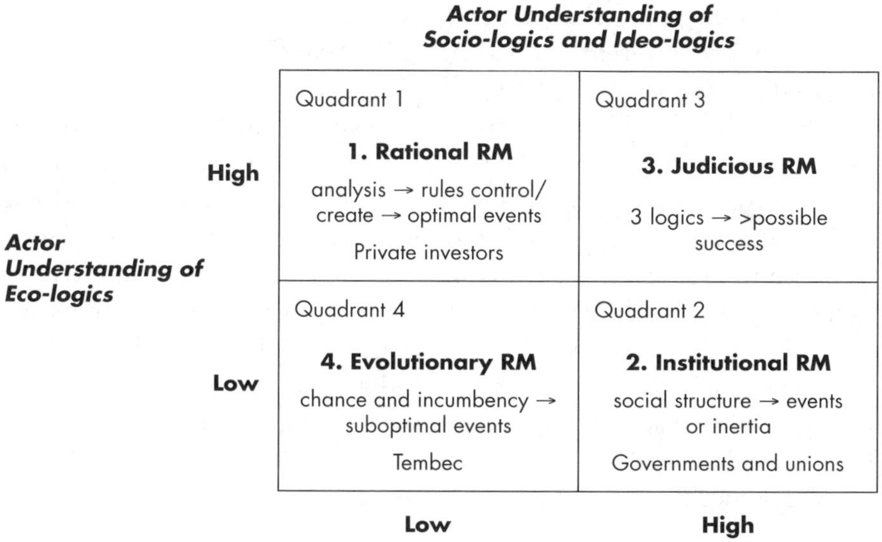

***Actor Understanding of
Socio-logics and Ideo-logics***

	Quadrant 1	Quadrant 3
High	**1. Rational RM** analysis → rules control/ create → optimal events Private investors	**3. Judicious RM** 3 logics → >possible success
Low	Quadrant 4 **4. Evolutionary RM** chance and incumbency → suboptimal events Tembec	Quadrant 2 **2. Institutional RM** social structure → events or inertia Governments and unions
	Low	**High**

*Actor
Understanding of
Eco-logics*

FIGURE 6.3 Gaspesia: Multiple Logics and Project Risk Management (RM)

Source: Vit (2010)

the evolution of chance events and reliance on past routines that culmi-nated in large unintended negative consequences. This idea of different framing by an appreciative system is firmly rooted in the dialogue of multiple economic and social logics proposed by Merton,[16] Thompson and Tudon,[17] Vickers,[18] Martinet,[19] and Lounsbury.[20]

Method

Empirical evidence will be presented in the form of an exploratory study, which will rely principally upon the testimony of over 55 witnesses in a Public Commission of Inquiry (Lesage 2005), as well as archival com-pany, government and project data.[21] Since only a French language version of the inquiry's report was produced, all quotes from the inquiry have been liberally translated into English.[22]

The commission of inquiry was undertaken by a new successor provin-cial government after a previous government was involved with major project decisions. As such, the final success of the project is open for reconstruction given that facts are selected, valued and acted upon differently by different individuals.[23,24] Nevertheless, the judiciaries involved have substantiated major facts by means of written documents and the testimony of key participants. I have principally relied upon the Lesage inquiry for the material simple facts and concrete events related to this project, including financing details, timing of events and the actions of major participants.[25] In addition, where possible, triangulation from multiple sources, such as company (Tembec), government lending agency (Quebec and Canada) and union (FTQ) financial statements and archival data, has been used to improve the reliability and validity of the data. The author has forest products industry and project finance experience and has had exposure to industry eco-logics. He has worked for large Canadian and American financial institutions and financed large forest products firms in Quebec for over a decade.

Historical Background: The Chandler Gaspe Mill, Quebec, Canada

An American investor, Percy Milton Chandler, built a sulfite pulp mill on the Gaspe Peninsula 50 miles west of Perce rock in 1915. A company town emerged, with over 450 workers employed at the local Chandler mill. The mill had technical problems and achieved 20,000 tons of its planned 40,000 ton capacity. It was sold to investors and went bankrupt in 1923. It was purchased by the Bonaventure Pulp and Paper Company in 1925 and again went bankrupt in 1931, as the 1929 crash and subsequent depression severely impacted paper markets. The pulp mill resumed operations in 1937, and in 1953 it was expanded to a capacity of 83,000 metric tons of kraft pulp per year. It employed over 500 workers and 80 percent of its production was exported to the USA. In 1961 the mill was acquired by the Price Brothers (51 percent equity control) and the *New York Times*. The *New York Times* (49 percent equity) also became its principal customer. The mill was converted into a newsprint mill and began production in 1963 with a capacity of 60,000 tons, and a second paper machine was added in 1968. In 1974 Abitibi Paper merged with Price paper and became the 51 percent owner of the mill. Investments were made to upgrade the mill and thermomechanical pulping was introduced. The cost of production increased vis-à-vis newer mills, and in 1994 the *New York Times* sold its stake to Abitibi. In 1997 Abitibi merged with Stone Paper, doubling its size. In a 1998 review of its facilities, the decision was made to close the Chandler mill in 1999 due to its high cost of production, outdated assets and newsprint industry overcapacity. This resulted in the lay-off of 500 workers and severely impacted the region, which was already suffering under a second moratorium imposed on cod fishing. On July 19, 2000, Abitibi sold the Chandler mill to the Fonds de solidarité des travailleurs du Quebec (FTQ), a union pension fund, for $35 million ($30 million for the property and $5 million for equipment). Abitibi also included an important non-compete clause that stipulated that the mill could not produce newsprint until 2010. Thus, the search began to create a new vocation for the Chandler mill.

The Gaspesia Mega-project Mega-failure

On September 28, 2001, the FTQ, Tembec Industries Inc. and a Quebec government development agency, SGF Rexfor Inc., signed a letter of intent to be associated with a new $465 million project, which included estimated construction costs of $350 million. The Chandler mill would be refurbished and produce a new product, high-quality coated paper no. 4. The annual capacity of the new mill was expected to be 200,000 tons. On December 17, 2001, the premier of Quebec and the presidents of the FTQ, Tembec and SGF Rexfor publicly announced the project would go ahead. Throughout 2002 and 2003 the project proceeded through various iterations, errors and deviations that will be outlined below. As previously noted, the project was abandoned on January 30, 2004, having been 40.7 percent completed. Various actions and unintended consequences created successive cost overruns that had driven the projected final cost to over $700 million. The partnership filed for protection from creditors on February 10, 2004, having lost over $312 million of mainly taxpayers' funds.

The Three Logics

The account above has set out the chronology of events surrounding the failure of a large project in Quebec in 2004. While the disentanglement of causes and effects is difficult, this chapter will rely upon the facts presented in the Quebec Provincial Commission of Inquiry into the Gaspesia Paper Project presided over by Judge Robert Lesage.[26]

Facts from the inquiry will be used to illustrate three packages of constructs. First, facts related to the underlying technical and economic logic of the project will be discussed. Second, cognitive routines and patterns of behavior that eclipse economic logic will be treated. Last, normative predispositions of different actors will be discussed. I call these eco-logics, socio-logics and ideo-logics, respectively.[27,28] Martinet has similarly noted that different schemas exist that result in multiple approaches to strategy and different approaches to problems.[29] Similar to eco-logics, and coordination by rules, he notes that an assumption of objectivity results in objective technical-economic problem solving approaches.[30,31] Similar to socio-logics and ideo-logics, he observes that an assumption of subjectivity results in subjective problem finding. Interaction between objectivity and subjectivity can also result in issues enacting approaches to problems that he calls constructivist. Martinet calls this management by rules, management by arguments and management by symbols, respectively.

An important contribution of this example is that different understandings of these multiple logics formed appreciative systems for project members that in most cases decoupled from the underlying technical and economic logic of the project.[32] I have called this mismanagement.[33]

Rational Risk Management

I call managing with technical and economic logic "rational risk management" and this is illustrated in Figure 6.4a. The brief history of the pulp and paper mill at Chandler outlined above has indicated that the paper industry has been relatively volatile over time and that successive predecessors in the private sector enjoyed significant risks and returns over the last 90 years. The town of Chandler remained a one-trick

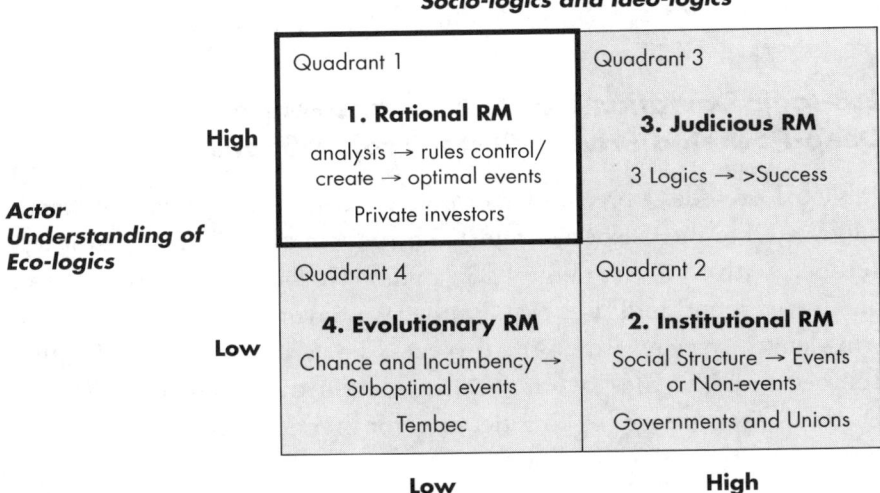

FIGURE 6.4a Rational-Technical Risk Management (RM)

Source: Vit (2010)

economic pony, and the pulp and paper mill assets were ancient when the FTQ purchased them for $35 million in 2000. Thus, a new project was created, with new technology for a new market, due to Abitibi's newsprint non-compete clause. This represented a major, very high-risk engineering undertaking.

The project evolved and deviated from very basic technical tenets of project finance and economics that I call eco-logics. Figure 6.4a highlights the case when a project actor relies upon eco-logics. Interestingly, there was little economic or technical understanding of the project by investors and there were many deviations from accepted eco-logics. Most private investors who examined the project passed on it. They found that the project deviated significantly from accepted technical rationality. John Hancock, the sole private investor to advance cash, lived with the uncertainty of not having a deep-pocketed project leader with significant capital at risk, and an unproven technology, due to its contractual economic senior creditor lending structure. Its rational risk management was incomplete and was narrowly limited to financial protection via a financial and legal contractual structure. All project participants had not understood fundamental technical aspects of the project. These deviations from economic logic are outlined below.

Eco-logic Deviation No. 1: No Arms-Length Deep-Pocketed Private Sector Project Sponsor(s)

Table 6.1 provides a breakdown of investor commitments and outstandings related to the Gaspesia project. The only initial private investor was Tembec, with an investment of $35 million. It is important to note that the Lesage report indicates that Tembec was favored in at least two non-arms-length ways regarding the project.[34] First, a $35 million debt that Tembec owed to the government in relation to a project in Matane, Quebec, was expunged as consideration for their investment in Gaspesia.

TABLE 6.1 Gaspesia Investors

Entity	Type of Investor	Committed	Disbursed as of 31/01/2004
Fonds de Solidarité	Partner Capital	$70,000,000	$70,000,000
SGF Rexfor	Partner Capital	$35,000,000	$35,000,000
Tembec	Partner Capital	$35,000,000	$35,000,000
Investment Quebec	Gov. Loan, No Interest	$145,250,000	$68,459,869
Economic Development Canada	Gov. Loan, No Interest	$80,000,000	$50,756,540
John Hancock	Private Sector Loan	$70,000,000	$23,947,600*
Inno-pap	Gov. Grant	$58,000,000	$28,852,379
TOTAL		$493,250,000	$358,016,388

Note: * $22.8 million of this amount was subsequently recovered by John Hancock due to its senior position in the financing, leaving Gaspesia creditors with cash assets of approx. $2 million and a 40.7% completed construction site.

Source: Vit (2010)

This consideration effectively made their cash contribution zero. Lesage notes:

> At the same time, Tembec, who was obliged to pay a penalty of $35 M to Investissement Quebec if it did not install a new paper machine in its factory in Matane, negotiated with the government not to pay this penalty.[35]

Second, a limited partnership structure that was created to promote and build the Gaspesia project appears to have no inherent logic other than to have been suggested by legal advisors as a means of saving Tembec taxes payable, since the other partnership members were not taxable. Lesage notes that the practice of a government entity aiding a private party to avoid taxes goes against the principle of taxpayer equity before the law; it may have saved Tembec a possible $19 million and earned law firms and accounting firms substantial legal and accounting fees for professional advice:

> Speculation? No: [it was] a realistic estimate, which was in accordance with the conventions of the parties and which influenced the involvement of specialists, lawyers and accountants . . . the important bills [of these contracts] were paid by Papiers Gaspesia, a sponsored corporation. At the core, this is a flagrant action not respecting the principles of taxpayer equity, a certain reward given by the government to a taxpayer.[36]

In addition, Tembec was a relatively small, high-risk company in 2000. Its 2000 annual report indicates that its long-term debt was rated BB+ by Standard & Poor's, which is equivalent to high-risk junk bond status.[37]

Furthermore, the project was not bankable in the private bank market, as no banks, foreign or domestic, would commit to the project on a stand-alone basis, and required guarantees from project sponsors during its capital-raising phase. Lesage quotes the testimony of Louis Lavigne, of Investissement Quebec, formerly called SGF:

> When a banker, ranked #1, asks the shareholders for a deposit, this means that the project is not profitable enough for a banker

without a deposit from shareholders to engage in the financing of the project.[38]

As discussed, one private institutional investor, John Hancock, did commit $70 million and had advanced $24 million when the project was halted. It was structurally a deeply senior secured creditor and also had recourse to the project sponsors. It was also the only entity that did not materially lose its investments in Gaspesia. Yet, it did not understand the technological and engineering risks of the project discussed below.

Eco-logic Deviation No. 2: Unproven Technology

According to Lesage, the nature of the underlying technology for the Gaspesia project represented significant technical risk.[39] The FTQ approached an engineering firm, BPR, which together with the world's largest producer of paper machines, Metso of Finland, developed the idea of producing high-quality coated paper no. 4 using new technology related to thermomechanical pulping. The underlying idea was that chemical pulping, while being superior in the quality of fiber produced, had significant environmental and operating costs. Most of the technology had been proven elsewhere for no. 5 paper, although Lesage noted that the Chandler mill would be the first paper mill in North America to use in-line super calenders, in one single large line, to endeavor to produce no. 4 paper.[40] This had never been attempted anywhere before; however, it seemed technically feasible, yet complex.

Eco-logic Deviation No. 3: Midstream Change of Project Scope and Project Engineers

BPR was hired to do in-depth feasibility engineering work on this idea on June 14, 2001. In December 2001 BPR was hired as the main engineering consultant for the project. Tembec was appointed project manager in September 2001 and suggested substantial changes to the scope of the project design in January 2002. BPR indicated that changes would increase the estimated project construction costs by $60 million from $350 million to $410 million, and would require significant additional engineering. Tembec and its partners ignored BPR's strong indications in this regard throughout February 2002, and on March 6, 2002, BPR was dismissed. A new alliance of two engineering firms, JP-ABSG, was hired that was totally unfamiliar with the project, which was in advanced stages of design. Interestingly, given the substantial technical and engineering firm changes to the project, the project partners stuck to their initial project cost and timetable projections, even though no analysis of the new engineering and construction phases of the project had yet been completed. In a detailed report on June 7, 2002, JP-ABSG also indicated that project construction costs would be at least $42 million greater than $350 million, and an independent engineering firm for the lenders, AMEC, also concluded in their due diligence report on August 14, 2002, that the construction expenditures of the project would cost in excess of $410 million and that major technical challenges and risks had to be overcome. Lenders finally stopped advancing funds after AMEC's seventh unfavorable report in January 2004.

Evolutionary Risk Management

Tembec was notionally the project leader, yet, as previously mentioned, it was weak financially and had not committed itself to the project in a meaningful way. Also, the ultimate responsibility for driving the project forward and for creating a detailed project and construction process was diffused. Given the unrealistic timetable and budget envisaged and repeatedly confirmed by Tembec and its partners, the new engineering firm refused to be responsible for monitoring construction progress, which was a major departure from accepted project finance practice. Tembec did not have the resources or capabilities to monitor the construction of the project, and overall leadership and responsibility for managing the project did not exist. Lesage notes that Miller and Lessard[41] suggest that the antithesis of this approach is required by a project sponsor, who should have significant "skin in the game":

> Ownership competencies. The prime competency of any sponsor is the ability to think, select, and behave as a responsible project owner who will have to operate the projects it builds. The obligation to make these tradeoffs forces it to challenge co-specialized parties and

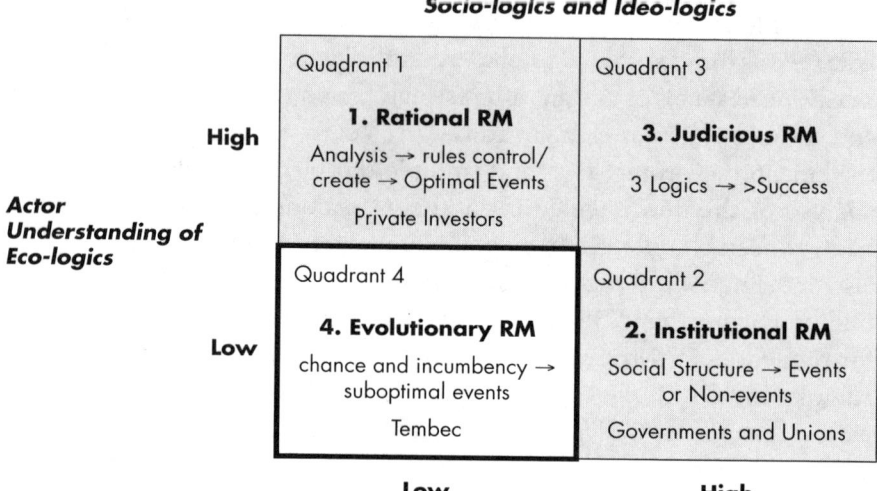

FIGURE 6.4b Evolutionary Risk Management (RM)

Source: Vit (2010)

contractors. The sponsor acts as a master contractor, paying for the project and living with the consequences of choices.[42]

Lesage observes that none of the project sponsors assumed this fundamental project finance responsibility throughout the project's short life (December 2001 to January 2004):

> Here, Papiers Gaspesia was not a responsible project owner. None of the partners took initiatives like a true entrepreneur. Tembec, in charge of the management of the project under contract paid by Papiers Gaspesia, had to offer operating advice and had to sell the product, all at the expense of Papiers Gaspesia. None of the three partners, Tembec, Rexfor and le Fonds, had any obligation in advance in case the project slipped in the wrong direction . . . In reality, this structure had no pilot (or leader) and if the project went badly, the citizen would have to endure the consequences: however, if the project went well, the private sector would profit from it. The public, represented by managers that are not strong leaders in the area, was thus taking all of the risk.[43]

Thus, the strictures of classical project finance eco-logics were not applied in the case of the Gaspesia project. Engineering firms were changed. Collaboration and coordination in the design and construction phase of the project with construction contractors, engineers and the ostensible project leader, Tembec, were minimal. A detailed construction plan did not exist when the project leader began construction. This resulted in strained labor relations, rushed timing and intransigence in recognizing obvious errors and overruns on the part of government partners to the project who were more intent upon maintaining legitimacy. Tembec in particular (Quadrant 4) did not fully understand the influence of social and normative forces upon economic rationality, or socio-logics and ideo-logics. I call this lack of understanding of all three logics "evolutionary risk management." The Riemann sum of small chance events and incumbent routines may add up to massive project losses. In this case, small latent errors and assumptions can result in large unintended consequences down the road. For example, Ramanujan and Goodman demonstrated that deviations in expectations related to trading execution, monitoring and infrastructure resulted in the demise of Barings bank.[44] In the case of Gaspesia, Tembec's misunderstanding of technical rationality and social and normative conditions allowed the project to drift and be buffeted by chance events and entrenched social routines, such as Tembec's past favorable dealings with government, that ultimately caused financial losses to escalate.

As previously noted, the Gaspesia project partners created a tax-motivated and diffuse limited partnership that had as its members Tembec, a forest products company, two government agencies, and government lenders. Commitments and outstandings (in $ millions) were, as shown in Table 6.1 (p. 72), above when the partnership filed for creditor protection.

Institutional Risk Management

I define socio-logics as cognitive routines that achieve a taken-for-granted sense that may either hinder the action of eco-logics by government actors or, conversely, actually facilitate expert decision-making due to experience and pattern recognition within a context such as managerial

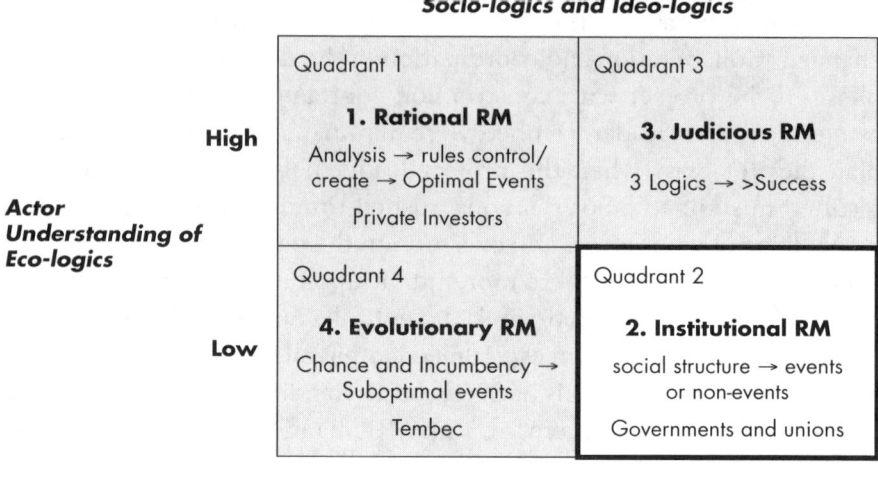

FIGURE 6.4c Institutional Risk Management (RM)

Source: Vit (2010)

decisions by private enterprises.[45,46,47] In the case of the private banking sector, one banker summarized the quick pass given to the Gaspesia project financing request by foreign and domestic banks as follows: "No bank would touch this deal . . . the deal structure, the project sponsor . . . technology . . . distance from markets, and players resulted in a high risk, marginal project based upon my experience of many pulp and paper projects."

The socio-logics of the government agency lenders and union pension fund and government partners were different. The FTQ is a $6.2 billion net asset value pension fund that invests union member as well as tax-incentivized pension plan investments from the Quebec public.[48] The fund invests principally in private sector job-creating developmental ventures in the province of Quebec. In the case of Gaspesia, project decisions and actions were more related to social isomorphism than economic isomorphism.[49] Union construction jobs were being created in the short run and hopefully mill-worker jobs in the long run.

Also, as elsewhere, strong norms and values I call ideo-logics run deep in Quebec unions. For example, Quebec is a highly unionized industrial setting with its own value systems. The construction industry enjoys legislation that results in closed-shop union protectionism. A priori, it seemed that having the FTQ as a 50 percent investor would smooth union relations, particularly with its own union, and expedite the project. In fact, Lesage indicates that the opposite happened as a lack of project planning, due to the aforementioned changes in engineering firms and the project scope, resulted in mass confusion at the project site and a sense of FTQ union entitlement that created major conflicts and intimidation between Tembec, private unionized contractors and rival unions within the mill.[50] For example, Lesage notes that 95 percent of workers on the site belonged to two unions which enjoyed quasi-monopoly power over decision making: "On Papiers Gaspesia's work-site, between April 29th and January 30th 2004, around 95% of the workers working there were part of the Conseil conjoint FTQ-construction and CPQMC-1."[51]

This union monopoly also had a major negative impact on productivity. For example, Lesage notes that the union successfully decreed that the work day would be cut from eight hours to five hours and twenty minutes of actual work:

> The double reality of a union quasi-monopoly . . . rapidly established a dominant culture and exclusivity on the work-site . . . Following the pressures from the union, the labor hours on the work-site were rearranged, causing lower productivity. In fact, starting in fall 2003, the workers were given a daily two hours and 40 minutes of paid leisure time (not working), leaving five hours and 20 minutes of actual labor productivity with a quarter of the work done in the afternoon lasting 35 minutes only.[52]

Labor problems and incidents multiplied as the construction of the new mill progressed. For example, Tembec's project manager resisted union pressures, and this resulted in a riot that caused its project manager to resign after over 400 angry workers surrounded his barricaded trailer on August 6, 2003, demanding his removal. Tembec's project manager surreptitiously left the site, never to return. In one other incident among many, angry construction workers refused to allow mill workers from a different union to unload the new paper machine that had arrived by sea from Finland.

The FTQ fund's president made representations to the partnership's board that his union would cooperate throughout the life of the project; however, this proved difficult due to a sense of entitlement and union monopoly enjoyed at the project site. It is interesting to note that in 1979 ITT corporation lost US$320 million on a pulp mill investment at Port Cartier across the St. Lawrence river from Gaspe due in part to militant unions and a lack of on-site due diligence. Shapira and Berndt have noted that project champions will reject all evidence related to comparable projects as incomparable in order to build legitimacy.[53]

The other two partners in the partnership were government agencies who also abdicated economic responsibility for the project. Lesage notes that SGF's CEO was not keen on the project yet was politically pressured to participate:

> As the ex-CEO mentioned, his initial reaction towards an investment from SGF in Gaspesia was negative, because [he believed that] such a project required the presence of major industrial partners, involved in the target market, with a historical record of success and sufficient capital. These were the guidelines that a "responsible" owner would follow. The Prime Minister . . . put pressure on the CEO.[54]

The same investor-truncated rationality existed within government lending agencies. For example, the federal government's Canadian Economic Development agency (CED) incurred loan losses of $50.7 million dollars when Gaspesia was terminated in January 2004. Notwithstanding this fact, CED has a detailed "logic model" flow chart in its performance report dated March 31, 2004, which assumes a rational analytic approach to development lending, including careful analysis. The report indicates that a thorough rational assessment of projects is made; yet within the same report it also indicates that its loan program is actually generally for small and medium-sized enterprises, and that its numbers have been distorted by the Gaspesia project.

The "performance" report discusses the $80 million commitment to Gaspesia as a loan commitment, but it does not suggest that the loan was an unmitigated disaster. Rather, the report is couched in shadow rationality and buzz words that build legitimacy. This social conformity and legitimacy-building behavior in the face of hard economic facts to the contrary is evidence of the power of conformist social forces within Gaspesia project partners even ex post a failed project. I call this reliance on non-economic logics institutional risk management.

Judicious Risk Management

Judicious or contrarian risk management depicts risk management wherein a project participant has insight into the technical and economic aspects of a project, as well as the social and normative forces at work (see Figure 6.4d). [55]

Some potential investors and partners in Gaspesia were aware of both the deviations in economic logic and the strong social and normative forces at work with unions and government bodies. No private investors participated in the project except for Tembec and John Hancock. They were both contractually protected from economic loss due to tax concessions and deal structure, respectively. However, both technical and

Actor Understanding of
Socio-logics and Ideo-logics

		Low	High
Actor Understanding of Eco-logics	**High**	**Quadrant 1** **1. Rational RM** Analysis → rules control/create → Optimal Events Private Investors	**Quadrant 3** **3. Judicious RM** 3 Logics → >Success
	Low	**Quadrant 4** **4. Evolutionary RM** Chance and Incumbency → Suboptimal events Tembec	**Quadrant 2** **2. Institutional RM** Social Structure → Events or Non-events Governments and Unions

FIGURE 6.4d Judicious (Contrarian) Risk Management (RM)

Source: Vit (2010)

social forces remained misunderstood and this resulted in the project's demise. This is evidence of evolutionary risk management, the antithesis of judicious risk management. Also, the government entities and unions involved had their own norms and social logics and engaged in institutional risk management, seemingly divorced from technical and economic engineering reports and red flags throughout the project's life. Successful project completion required a deep understanding of all logics.

Discussion

It is useful to examine how economic sense is overridden by social and ideological forces at both the organizational and the institutional levels of analysis. Both institutional and configuration theory suggest that organizations achieve coordination via conformity by using dominant accepted eco-logics. Work at Gaspesia was supposed to be coordinated by the standardization of norms, work processes and outputs, and expert skills. The inaction of many of these mechanisms was visible within Gaspesia's partner and lender organizations, and also within the new entity, the Gaspesia Limited Partnership.

Engineering design, which normally standardizes work processes and output prior to construction in consultation with construction contractors due to technological complexity, was actually not completed in the case of Gaspesia when the project got under way and thousands of construction workers were on the job site. Lesage has noted that the resulting chaos was due in part to rushed timing by inexperienced project partners, Tembec's failure to provide sufficient personnel and expertise on-site and, most significantly, a change in project scope and engineers. The new engineers provided expert knowledge via their standardized professional skills, yet they refused to supervise and sign off on project costs as they unfolded, due to informational opaqueness and the lack of a construction critical path and detailed plan.

Coordination via the standardization of norms was also difficult to achieve. The union movement enjoyed a closed shop construction site advantage that had its origins in the nineteenth century in Quebec. The FTQ had its own performance norms that differed from those of the private sector. Politicians and government bureaucrats were also interested in job preservation as a performance norm, including their own jobs. Tembec, a private sector company, was a highly indebted high-risk firm that had turned around other mills with government help and had not committed sufficient resources or manpower to manage the project site.

Strong social and ideological support on the part of many project sponsors overrode technical and economic considerations and caused the Gaspesia project to fail. As discussed above, the capital providers of the project were mainly government agencies and a union pension fund.

Conclusion

This chapter has important managerial and policy implications for actors within organizations. The Gaspesia project's failure demonstrates how reasonable actors within private and public organizations became entangled in different logics and risk management that trumped economic sense. The chapter offers a guide to practitioners, since it highlights how social sense was managed and mismanaged during the signaling of escalating project engineering and financial problems. As public–private partnerships have become a more prevalent emerging organizational form, care must be exercised in clearly understanding and delineating economic logic and project leadership from competing logics.

Managers will note that Gaspesia's history, position in its environment, and the unintended consequences of the actions of government and private sector managers are evidence of a veneer of economic rationality. The unique socio-logics and ideo-logics of the major project participants drove their aspirations and the project forward since their survival was never at risk. Facts were heavily filtered and selected by government agencies. In the case of Gaspesia, socio-logics and ideo-logics overrode economic rationality or eco-logics. Practitioners may now benefit from being aware that these logics drove the project forward and downward.

Researchers and students of organizations may also be able to use the proposed framework to further their understanding of project and financial meltdowns. More specifically, this chapter uses an application of the Holistic Risk Management Model (HRMM) which combines four complementary views of risk management that seek to explain how a risky situation developed. Project actors used different organizational and institutional logics that formed an appreciative system of rational, evolutionary, institutional and judicious risk management processes. These are illustrated in this case study and contribute to our conceptual understanding of a project's failure. This is further reinforced at higher levels of analysis by mimetic government institutions and unions.

This study builds upon the growing body of case studies that have examined the escalation of commitment to projects. It further demonstrates how different mechanisms, such as the rules, cognitive routines and ideological pressures of an institutional environment, wove together to paradoxically eclipse the technical and economic rationality of actors within these organizations. This abdication and override of technical rationality masquerading as innovation continues to manifest itself in many surprising and highly negative ways which provide fertile avenues of future research.

Thus, this chapter has provided a broad framework that describes how institutional and evolutionary risk management disconnected attention to rational risk management in the Gaspesia project. In addition to over $312 million in real losses, this resulted in severe financial and social consequences for the people of Chandler, a small town in Gaspe, Quebec, Canada. Risk taking and government involvement in project finance must be viewed in the context of the multiple processes and logics that were illustrated by the application of the HRMM to this project failure.

Chapter 7

Contrarian Risk Management

Case 5: The UBS Sub-prime Meltdown and Case 6: The Société Générale Fraud

Chapter Summary

This chapter will focus upon two cases of runaway risk taking that resulted in large losses for two financial institutions, Union Bank of

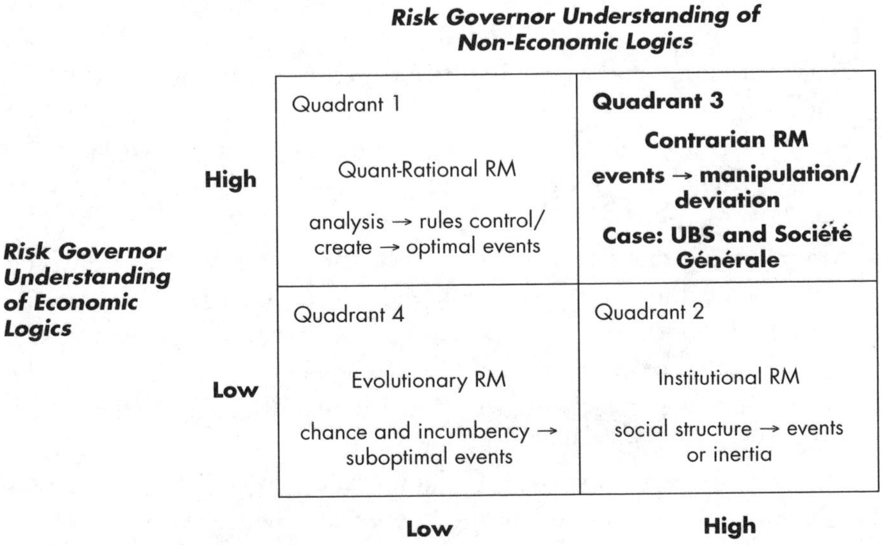

Risk Governor Understanding of Non-Economic Logics

	High	Quadrant 1 Quant-Rational RM analysis → rules control/ create → optimal events	**Quadrant 3** **Contrarian RM** **events → manipulation/** **deviation** **Case: UBS and Société** **Générale**
Risk Governor Understanding of Economic Logics	**Low**	Quadrant 4 Evolutionary RM chance and incumbency → suboptimal events	Quadrant 2 Institutional RM social structure → events or inertia
		Low	**High**

FIGURE 7.1 The Holistic Risk Management Model (HRMM)—Contrarian Risk Management

Switzerland (UBS) and Société Générale (SocGen). Both cases involved massive risk taking by rainmaking elites. At SocGen this led to fraud, and at UBS it led to financial mismanagement and financial deception.

In the case of the two banks discussed below, contrarian in-groups used the social space created by their understanding of economic and non-economic logics in order to deviate and profit from conformity.

The UBS and Société Générale Cases

This chapter presents more preliminary research on competing economic, social and ideological forces that I have represented as the Holistic Risk Management Model (HRMM). The granular preliminary data contained in this chapter is principally taken from a shareholder report on UBS's write-downs that is represented as a reasonable summary of a report that outlined UBS's problems for the Swiss Federal Banking Commission.[1,2]

For Société Générale (SocGen), internal auditor data was principally obtained from internal progress reports of the Special Committee of the Board of Directors of Société Générale dated February 20, 2008, and May 20, 2008, which were made public. The committee, in turn, relied upon summary reports of interim conclusions produced by the General Inspection Department of the bank called "Mission Green" dated February 20, 2008 and May 23, 2008, which were also disclosed to the public.[3]

Further reports by auditors, government authorities and legal authorities may provide more interesting data in the future. Although the data is still incomplete, important preliminary observations can begin to be drawn regarding risk management at UBS and Société Générale which are discussed below.[4] It is also recognized that SocGen and UBS internal and external reports contain inherent biases; however, this chapter will demonstrate that preliminary conclusions can begin to be made from the facts that have been presented to date.[5] The National Australia Bank chapter has tracked a similar phenomenon, a derivatives trading debacle, in Australia's largest bank using similar methods, and similar conclusions can be drawn regarding the failure of quant risk management.

UBS

As noted, recently large banks have engaged in seemingly carefully calcu-lated risk taking that has in fact jeopardized their existence. For example, in 2007 and 2008 Union Bank of Switzerland AG (UBS) suffered spectacular losses (over US$53 billion), which were related to US real estate exposure. Its market capitalization declined from SFR154 billion at December 31, 2006, to SFR43 billion at December 31, 2008, which was close to the book value of its equity. Such wealth destruction is unprecedented. UBS will be used as a proxy to describe what happened in many financial institutions that suffered large write-downs and losses (i.e. AIG, Citibank, Merrill Lynch and Lehman Brothers). I will then describe fraudulent risk management deviation activities at SocGen that are strikingly similar.

In June 2005 UBS created an internal hedge fund, Dillon Read Capital Management (DRCM), with attractive compensation for its fund man-agers within its Global Asset Management business.[6] At this time UBS also appointed a new head of its Investment Banking (IB) Group. The new head of IB commissioned external consultants to conduct a strategy review of its businesses, and the consultants noted several major "revenue gaps" in its businesses.[7] UBS was compared to the top three bank "leaders in revenues" by different activities, and the consultants concluded that UBS had deficiencies in Credit, Securitized Products and Commodities businesses.

In March 2006 IB proposed a new set of growth strategies to senior UBS management, which were approved. It recommended fixed income growth initiatives in securitized products, commercial real estate capital markets, high yield and structured credit. The new internal hedge fund, DRCM, took over the trading of many of these instruments in 2006, and they were responsible for approximately one-third of UBS's write downs and losses to date.[8] The other main contributor to UBS's losses (similar to AIG's US$105 billion in write-offs) was its activities related to collat-eralized debt obligations, CDOs. UBS was exposed to huge risk through the IB CDO desk's origination and underwriting business. UBS, however, did not have a cap on the total amount of CDO activity permitted.

UBS notes: "Throughout 2006 and 2007, there were no aggregate notional limits on the sum of the CDO Warehouse pipeline and retained pipeline positions."[9] This lack of limits on overall exposure is a major deviation and is similar to the absence of limits on foreign exchange contracts by SocGen that resulted in Jerome Kerviel being able to actually go long and then fictively go short €20 billion, thus showing no apparent risk from his new position. As with AIG, the focus of models related to CDO was on the probability of default. Data used relatively recent time series and was time weighted even more recently using quant models. Thus, default probabilities in the boom phase of a real estate cycle were deemed to be very low.

UBS continued to add to its super senior CDO assets in 2007 because they believed that the credit risk of their investments was backstopped by AAA credit ratings, which were in part due to insurance company guarantors. They neither questioned the strength of these insurers and structures (relying upon rating agency ratings) until they evaporated, and nor did they seek to "look through" structures at underlying toxic real estate assets, or to "look up" at rapidly rising markets. UBS's "proprietary" fixed income business described above was also fueled by over US$100 billion in off-market low-cost parent funding that further subsidized profitability.[10]

Société Générale

On January 18 and 20, 2008, a French bank, Société Générale (SocGen), discovered large unauthorized directional positions in one of its equities derivatives groups, Delta One. A rogue trader was questioned, dismissed and subsequently convicted of fraudulent activities. The total loss to SocGen on closing out the positions amounted to €4.9 billion (approx US$7.2 billion) when they were eliminated by the bank in trading in a declining market on January 21 and 23, 2008.

The mechanics of the organization's risk management systems, and in particular its responses to multiple massive signs that something had been amiss for over two years, are perhaps more interesting to explore than the alleged fraud itself. Such a large loss was a shock to the organization since it had highly advanced mathematical and technical systems to monitor risk.[11] At times, positions taken by one trader (i.e. approximately €49 billion in January 2008, see page 2 of the SocGen General

Inspection Department report of May 20, 2008) threatened the bank's survival since they equalled the market capitalization of the bank (approximately €49 billion) and far exceeded the book value of the bank's equity and reserves.[12] Why and how did these many risk management systems fail? This chapter will highlight the dialogue between economic and non-economic logics that help explain this failure.

Multiple Logics

The preliminary observations of the UBS and SocGen boards of directors as manifested in the above-mentioned data will be utilized to demonstrate the decoupling of economic rationality by non-economic logics. To begin with, facts related to the underlying technical and economic logic of risk systems at UBS and SocGen will be discussed. Mindless organizational routines, habits and patterns of behavior that trump economic logic will be treated as well. The chapter will also endeavor to discuss the different norms of the actors involved, although little data is available and further research is necessary in this regard. As discussed earlier, I call these multiple logics eco-logics, socio-logics and ideo-logics respectively.[13] All of these logics manifested themselves at UBS and SocGen at different times and within different groups. They combine with different levels of understanding to create quite different risk management processes that are represented at an organizational level in Figure 7.1.

Quadrant 1 of Figure 7.1 represents the case when risk governors (i.e. managers) are able to coordinate complex work using rules and routines, with low reliance upon understanding social and ideological logics. Figure 7.2 shows that many levels of control existed at UBS and SocGen (although they both failed to detect the innocent fraud and fraud, respectively, for a long time), and Table 7.1 illustrates the many rules and procedures that controlled risk at UBS and SocGen.

Quadrant 2 of Figure 7.1 suggests that risk governors, such as the SocGen Delta Group and UBS NY CDO traders' immediate superiors, understood and identified with the social and ideological mores of the trading group. This allowed them to focus on rituals and rewards for profit while being decoupled from and not understanding the technical

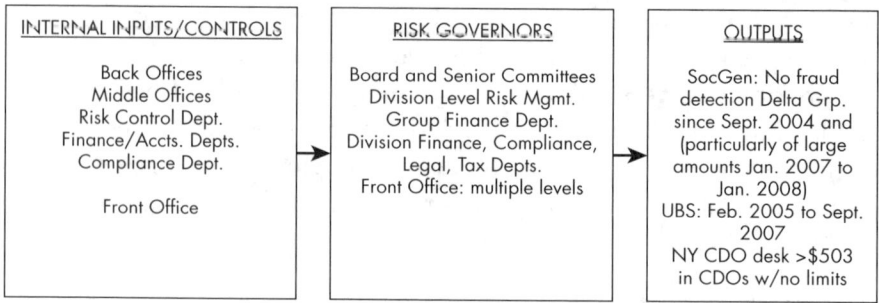

INTERNAL INPUTS/CONTROLS	RISK GOVERNORS	OUTPUTS
Back Offices Middle Offices Risk Control Dept. Finance/Accts. Depts. Compliance Dept. Front Office	Board and Senior Committees Division Level Risk Mgmt. Group Finance Dept. Division Finance, Compliance, Legal, Tax Depts. Front Office: multiple levels	SocGen: No fraud detection Delta Grp. since Sept. 2004 and (particularly of large amounts Jan. 2007 to Jan. 2008) UBS: Feb. 2005 to Sept. 2007 NY CDO desk >$503 in CDOs w/no limits

FIGURE 7.2   Eco-logics and Rational Risk Management Failure at SocGen and UBS

Source: Vit (2006)

rationality behind the trading and the fraudulent activity nested therein. At UBS, the head of Investment Banking used consultants to identify so-called revenue gaps in fixed income offerings versus the competition. Table 7.1 contrasts the stated economic logics at SocGen and UBS with the non-economic logics (socio-logics and ideo-logics) highlighted by the investigative reports.

SocGen and UBS risk governors were firmly relying on management by numbers in Quadrant 1 of Figure 7.1. They did not understand the damage to the technical efficiency of their economic systems as they were overridden by trader in-group cultures. Quadrant 4 of Figure 7.1 may also be at work, as it suggests that risk governor ignorance of both economic rationality and social and ideological pressures may allow small chance events and the Riemann sum of many small meaningless organizational routines to combine to create big suboptimal events such as a fraud or trading excesses that could threaten the survival of the organization. For example, armies of managers at SocGen and UBS were locked in their day-to-day algorithmic routines and not concerned with massive notional volumes being put on by traders in proprietary trading groups.

Economic Logic Failure at UBS and SocGen

Risk managers at UBS and SocGen relied upon sophisticated mathematical models to control risk via rational quantitative risk management models. This process is Cartesian as risks are anticipated, and rules are

TABLE 7.1 HRMM Risk Logics and Deviation at Société Générale and UBS

HRMM GENERIC	Economic Logics	Social Logics	Cultural Logics
Coordinating Mechanisms	(a) Mother banks: standardization of work processes and outputs specialists, reinforced by consultants and rating agencies	(a) Trader in-groups: Standardization of skills: opaque models	(a) Standardization of norms
Conformist Mechanisms	(a) Rational rules; (b) Economic models; (c) Algorithms; (d) Quantitative methods	(a) Cognitive routines; (b) Recipes; (c) Ceremonies	(a) Common values, norms/ identification (b) Internalization/ loyalty
Contrarian Deviation in Mechanisms	(a) Technology tampering (SG) (b) Alleged trader fraud, and alleged forgery of confirmations, trades and reports (SG) (c) New quant trading groups	(a) Exploiting rules (b) Reinforcing ceremony (c) Navigation within rules and hierarchies	(a) Cultural cleavages (b) In-groups vs. out groups

SocGen and UBS Bank RM Logics

	Economic Logics	Social Logics	Cultural Logics
Conformist Logics	I.e. SocGen Risk Division: (a) Defines and validates the methods used to analyze, assess, approve	SocGen ex post reports: (a) Lack of audit independence (b) Lack of escalation procedures	Declared values: Professionalism, team spirit and innovation SocGen 2007 Regulatory Report

TABLE 7.1 continued

HRMM	Economic Logics	Social Logics	Cultural Logics
	and monitor credit risks, country risks, market risks and operational risks (b) Conducts a critical review of sales strategies for high-risk areas and permanently seeks to improve the forecasting and management of all such risks (c) Contributes to the independent assessment by validating credit risk transactions and by taking position on obligors proposed by sales managers (d) Identifies all group risks and monitors the adequacy and consistency of risk management information systems I.e. UBS Risk	(c) Profits made/ bonuses paid without questioning (d) No superior oversight (e) Limits routinely exceeded (f) No cashflow tracking of large amounts (g) No contract limit tracking of large positions I.e. Report of the Special Committee of the Board of Directors of SocGen May 23, 2008, p. 3, weaknesses highlighted: (a) Difference between the growth in the means . . . to control and support services and the very strong growth in transaction volumes (b) Lack of certain controls liable to identify the fraudulent mechanisms, such as the control of	UBS: three keys symbolism (logo) SocGen unwritten norms: (a) Reward focus, not risk (b) Illusion of control (c) No need to escalate (d) Systems cannot keep up with volume (e) Trust traders (f) Highly hierarchical and bureaucratic SocGen: French social structure Educational system: Meritocratic elitism, senior executives selected from top schools which control entry based upon highly competitive entrance exam system UBS: social structures In-group US hedge fund/prop. trading US professionals/

HRMM	Economic Logics	Social Logics	Cultural Logics
	Management and Control: (a) Similar to above in 2007 (b) Reliance on rating agencies AAA ratings of super senior tranches of CDOs	the positions' nominal value or the transactions used (c) Fragmentation of controls between several units, with an insufficiently precise division of tasks, lack of systematic centralization of reports and of feedback to the appropriate hierarchical level I.e. UBS Risk Management and Control: deficiencies noted in 2008 by UBS Risk and Treasury Management: "UBS identified weaknesses in its risk management and control organization as well as limitations in its traditional market risk, credit risk, liquidity risk and funding risk measures (including the interplay between these measures . . . the firm failed to adequately address correlated risks, and risk concentrations"	hired guns. 3/30 Compensation large upside/no downside, and immediate

TABLE 7.1 continued

HRMM	Economic Logics	Social Logics	Cultural Logics
Contrarian Deviation in Logics	SocGen: (a) Technology tampering (b) Trade cancellations (c) Fictive trades and reporting UBS: (a) me-too strategy from consultants to close revenue gaps (b) creation of internal hedge fund with huge mgr incentives (c) availability of cheap parent $100 billion funding to internal hedge fund (d) no exposure limits (e) no "look through" to underlying assets UBS and SocGen: (a) Inter-bank/ proprietary trading strategy	SocGen (a) Approvals routinely obtained for excesses (b) Trader hierarchy of command ignored alerts, breaches and did not adequately review MIS output SocGen and UBS (a) no limits for massive positions and balance sheet risk	UBS and SocGen (a) Profits rewarded blindly; (b) Avoid escalation; (c) Limited identification; (d) Trader cults UBS ex post: Reinforced quantitative controls: expected loss, statistical loss and stress tests Reinforced qualitative controls: due diligence, sound judgment, common sense and an appreciation of a wide range of potential outcomes, including a willingness to challenge assumptions

Sources: Vit (2006); SocGen (2007a,b; 2008a,b) (http://www.societegenerale.fr/); PricewaterhouseCoopers (2008) (http://www.pwc.com/ca/en/index.jhtml); UBS (2008a,b; 2009a,b,c) (http://www.ubs.com/ca/en.html); SEC (2008; 2009) (http://www.sec.gov/)

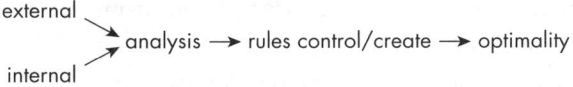

FIGURE 7.3 Quant-Rational Risk Management

Source: Vit (2009)

created to flag breaches and deviations from the norm. Quadrant 1 of the Holistic Risk Management Model describes this process (see Figure 7.3).

UBS

UBS described their classical planning model and its inability to explain the large sub-prime investment write-offs as follows:

> The 5 year strategic focus as articulated in the 5 Year Plan for 2007–2011 confirmed the previous year's trend of double-digit top-line increases . . . UBS at a group level focused on initiatives that were intended to further implement the integrated business model and grow businesses in line with UBS's longstanding focus on its three global core businesses. There was not, at the Group level, a particular and specific decision either to develop business in, or to increase exposure to, Subprime markets. Additionally, there was no specific decision substantially to increase UBS's overall risk taking in connection with these growth initiatives.[14]

Nevertheless, exposures grew exponentially in US sub-prime debt and, as previously noted, UBS has written off over $53 billion to date as they incurred trading losses when prices went down and wrote off loans when defaults went up. This was not planned for.

There exist implicit assumptions behind quant risk management, as discussed earlier in this book. First, the above assumes that the quant risk management model always has predictive power. Second, the model is top down and hierarchical. Success may be attributed to this activity, yet may have little to do with it. Third, numbers are relied upon and risk management is aggregated and formalized. Soft data and holistic approaches are largely ignored. Fourth, the quant model is temporal-centric and USA-centric as it is often promoted by US business schools and management and accounting consultants.

Third parties were also encouraged to invest in a second fund open to outsiders, and this resulted in complex reporting and UBS oversight that was different than if DRCM was simply a unit of UBS. UBS provided $100 billion in below-market cost funding and the fund initially bought and resold packages of US real estate loans.

Société Générale

SocGen's problems suggest that contingent events and incumbent routines eclipsed economic logic. For example, while derivative trading in a large bank involves thousands of transactions daily, the SocGen General Inspection Department report of May 20, 2008, noted that over 76 important alerts were tripped in the bank's systems by the rogue trader. Although technical procedures were followed, no one questioned or understood the magnitude of the trading positions even though the machines were signaling that large risks were being taken. Contrary to the bank's original assertions that a lone trader defrauded the bank by deceit and fraud that was undetectable, the banks rules and procedures as well as external parties tripped loud alarm bells within the bank that were ignored at multiple levels. This is illustrated in Figure 7.2 and Table 7.1 above. Hierarchies trumped markets and efficiency for over two years. For example, between March and November 2007 SocGen's OPER, GED, PNL, REC, ACFI, ACR, FCO departments, which controlled gateways for large money flows in and out of the bank, generated 13 alerts showing significant discrepancies including two transactions booked with (unknown at the time) fictional counterparties for a nominal value of €7 billion discovered by agent 29 on July 7.[15] The following explanation was given in the Inspection Department report as to why controls did not allow the fraud to be detected:

> Procedures were followed but no initiative was taken to verify the truth of JK's assertions and of the corrections suggested by him, even when these lacked probability. The next level of superiors failed to react when notified.[16]

PricewaterhouseCoopers adds:

> The Flaws revealed in the design, implementation and supervision of
> controls reduced their effectiveness vis a vis the fraud. In terms of
> design, the shortcomings of the system were apparent at several levels
> . . . As controls were split between several different units within the
> same function or sometimes between different functions, and because
> procedures were insufficiently explicit, this made it difficult to obtain
> an overview of the situation and gain an appropriate insight into the
> exceptions identified. The lack of a systematic procedure for centralis-
> ing and escalating red flags to the appropriate level in the organisation
> further exacerbated the problem. Procedures did not appropriately
> reflect the requirement in the group directive to analyse consistency
> of risks, results and positions. In practice, this role, which would have
> enabled an overview of the operations of Delta One Listed Products
> desk, was not carried out. Additionally there is no explicit reference
> to the monitoring of cash flows as a component of the internal control
> system which could have represented an additional red flag arising
> from the level of genuine activity of this desk.[17]

It is also interesting to observe the profits reported by Kerviel, the
rogue trader, versus the actual financial gains and losses that resulted
from his trading as outlined in Figure 7.4. Interestingly, from March to
July of 2007 the trader actually accumulated a large position on the
DAX index in excess of €30 billion and the bank had losses on positions
of approximately €2.5 billion, yet major alarm bells signaling something
was amiss were ignored. In fact, exhibit 6 of the report cites 78 alerts in
2007 and early 2008 that were material and could have resulted in the
fraud being detected, had many of them been acted upon. The trader
gave nonsensical explanations for discrepancies and red flags were not
acted upon. For example, on January 8, 2008, agent 3 asked for explanations regarding suspicious positions and received this reply from the
trader: "This materializes the give up of puts made late, I owe money to
the counterparty. It will be rebooked ASAP." In a subsequent interview
agent 3 admits not having understood the explanation.

Finally, an administrator, agent 27, after the involvement of over 40
administrators, took control of the case and suggested calling Bank C's

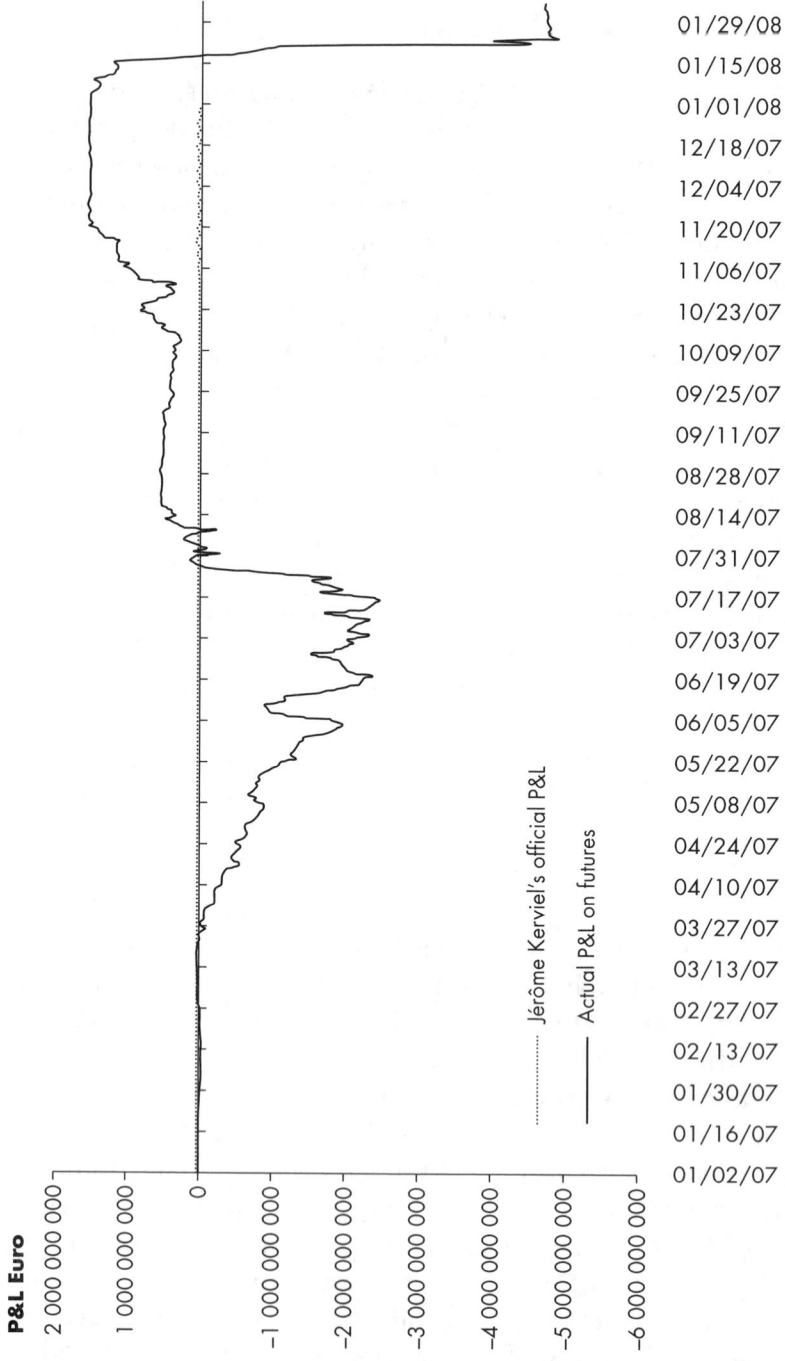

P&L Euro

....	Jérôme Kerviel's official P&L
——	Actual P&L on futures

01/29/08
01/15/08
01/01/08
12/18/07
12/04/07
11/20/07
11/06/07
10/23/07
10/09/07
09/25/07
09/11/07
08/28/07
08/14/07
07/31/07
07/17/07
07/03/07
06/19/07
06/05/07
05/22/07
05/08/07
04/24/07
04/10/07
03/27/07
03/13/07
02/27/07
02/13/07
01/30/07
01/16/07
01/02/07

2 000 000 000
1 000 000 000
0
−1 000 000 000
−2 000 000 000
−3 000 000 000
−4 000 000 000
−5 000 000 000
−6 000 000 000

FIGURE 7.4 Jerome Kerviel's Profit and Loss

Source: Société Générale (2008a,b)

trader (a counterparty) on a weekend to confirm whether trades were made since he knew the trader. As illustrated in Table 7.1 above, it is also interesting to note that a major common alarm bell did not exist. There was no control over total contract limits.[18]

Risk Management and Social Structure

As we saw in the institutional fortress that is Canadian banking, the weight of social structure influences risk management. Economic logic may matter less than social position. For example, senior executives at SocGen in France are often selected from top educational institutions in France, although this was not the case with Kerviel. Admittance to these schools is largely on the basis of successful performance in highly competitive entrance examinations. This creates a senior cadre of managers based upon a system of meritocratic elitism. Over half of France's 40 largest companies are run by executives from two schools which are renowned for training engineers and politicians, and together produce about only 600 graduates per year. Captains of industry, in turn, have strong social networks based in part upon this educational affiliation.[19] Also, the members of UBS's management board were historically mainly Swiss and longstanding UBS employees. The interlocking of boards was common, and educational and military service affiliations were tight. Similar to Canada, industry structure remains oligopolistic in both Switzerland and France and may have, until recently, provided a social buffer against the short-term global trading market discourses of quant models and money trading machines.

Bubble Trouble and Theory

UBS and SocGen both cite the explosion of volume and complexity in an up-market as a reason that systems lagged and failed.

The Holistic Risk Management Model, made up of three groups of nested logics (economic logics, social cognitive logics and cultural logics), can once again be applied to mutually reinforcing institutional, organizational and meta-business cycle levels of analysis, to track the evolution and ascendancy of small, powerful groups of insiders who made large concentrated bets in complex and opaque markets and models such as those related to the sub-prime debt mania. These three groups of constructs, technical economic analysis, social taken-for-grantedness and cultural predispositions, are present and active at these various levels of analysis across time. This chapter has mainly focused on an organizational level of analysis, using the two cases of UBS and SocGen.

One outcome of these processes is that sometimes organizations attribute successful causality to contingent or incumbent suboptimal events or even fraud, as this chapter demonstrates.[20] Thus, for a limited and very profitable time, risk governors and risk takers such as traders are compensated for their capacity to successfully go along with predictions of the random and unpredictable, and will bet large resources to achieve a bonus aspiration level when their survival is not at risk.

Chapter 8

Conclusions Regarding the Risk in Risk Management

The Holistic Risk Management Model

The Holistic Risk Management Model (HRMM) suggests that different logics are prominent at different times and act to create financial bubbles and accelerate two events: social override of economic rationality and crashes (see Figure 1.1). This is best represented by the cases and chapters in this volume.

Risk Governor Understanding of Non-Economic Logics

		Low	High
Risk Governor Understanding of Economic Logics	**High**	**Quadrant 1** **Quant-Rational RM** analysis → rules control/ create → optimal events	**Quadrant 3** **Contrarian RM** events → manipulation/ deviation **Cases: Parmalat, SocGen and UBS**
	Low	**Quadrant 4** **Evolutionary RM** chance and incumbency → suboptimal events **Cases: National Australia Bank, Gaspesia**	**Quadrant 2** **Institutional RM** social structure → events or inertia **Case: Canadian Banking**

FIGURE 8.1 The Holistic Risk Management Model (HRMM)

Within organizations and sub-groups, organizational theory is useful in understanding how certainty about uncertain risks and risk management methods intentionally and unintentionally builds legitimacy within organizations.[1,2,3,4,5,6,7,8] In particular, the HRMM (see Figure 8.1 above) illustrates that contrarian in-groups benefited from understanding the emergence and interplay of powerful organizational conformist processes. These nested logics involve the standardization of different norms and discourses across time and space, as well as different organizational cognitive routines and decision rules.[9,10,11,12,13]

Forecasting Conformity

The central idea of this volume has been to shed light upon a paradox in risk management. While some academics and practitioners are beginning to examine the economic sociology of risk management, significant time, effort and print continues to be spent upon building legitimacy for arcane dominant risk management models that often simply do not work. Their failure may be due to the non-economic social reasons mentioned throughout this volume that contribute to conformist approaches to risk. This volume questions the atomistic utility of the dominant "risk management model" as it appears in many business school risk management texts and major consultancies. It has highlighted the implicit and questionable assumptions behind this model and has suggested alternative lines of thinking about risk that should be treated in research, teaching and practice.

The All-Pervasive Conformist and Prescriptive Risk Management Model

Very real physical, operational, reputational and economic risks exist within and around organizations. It is important to note that these risks are very necessary to consider and manage, but may be eclipsed by social forces. This book has demonstrated that non-economic logics often hijack organizations, and economic logic dominates teaching and consultancy approaches to risk management. As discussed earlier, many

FIGURE 8.2 The Dominant Quant Risk Management Model

Source: Vit (2009)

practitioner-based approaches that endeavor to teach risk management at the undergraduate or MBA level still rely heavily upon a prescriptive economic analysis–formulation–implementation approach, as illustrated in Figure 8.2.

This dominant model has been institutionalized within many business schools and manifests itself in the discourse that surrounds "risk management" that is sold by large accounting firms and consultancies.[14] One way of illustrating the pervasiveness of the model is to look at how risk management is treated in bank annual reports and practitioner texts on the topic. Conventional risk management approaches that are used by many banks and business schools, and are manifested in risk management policies and procedures manuals and texts, follow similar formats and cover similar ground. Most approaches include sections that deal with analysis and ticking boxes. As shown in the Holistic Risk Management Model, the quant RM (risk management) model often includes "strategic" risk assessment employing strategy formulation that uses a SWOT analysis (strengths, weaknesses, opportunities, threats) and then strategy implementation.[15] A chapter is often entitled "external analysis" and exhorts neophytes and experienced managers alike to predict unpredictable trends related to externalities beyond the boundaries of the organization.[16,17]

Another chapter usually treats some form of internal analysis. Strengths and weaknesses are analyzed across functional areas and for the organization across business units and as a whole.[18,19] More recently, a resource-based view of the firm has emerged that includes an analysis of organizational tangible and intangible resources and their combination into capabilities.[20] Invincible capabilities are called core competencies, which must be rare, valuable, non-substitutable and imperfectly imitable. These are said to add value and create many years of sustainable growing cash flows and wealth. Incompetency is outsourced. Yet these advantages may be relatively short-lived.[21] Others have argued that in industries such as financial services all is imitable.[22] Other less perfect market contexts, such as market manias and bubbles, family-controlled businesses, visible and invisible cartels and market failures, are ignored.

Other parts of conventional risk management texts and manuals focus on topical subjects such as Corporate Governance and Ethics. The role of the board of directors, its composition and its involvement with "top" management are treated. There is also a focus upon implementation and control. This is often manifested in something called "organizational structure," accompanied by many uniform boxes connected by lines called organizational charts. Vital power relationships are invisible and not discussed. Another chapter or section of the generic risk management manual or text invariably looks at how controls can be put in place that will ensure that previous chapters or sections are successfully implemented. These involve MBO (management by objective) metrics that are based upon mainly financial controls and more recent questionable "modern" management techniques.[23,24] These are sometimes compared to untested "best practices" and standards.[25]

Thus, the risk management practitioner and student are exposed to reductionist frameworks, checklists and generic recipes without questioning their underlying taken-for-grantedness or effectiveness. It is useful to review some of the many implicit assumptions that exist behind this dominant model that could be made explicit.[26,27,28]

Making Implicit Risk Management Model Assumptions Explicit

First, the dominant quant risk management model and accompanying texts are highly prescriptive. It is assumed that if managers use the above framework, they will be more competitive and achieve greater shareholder wealth creation than those that use other methods. Evidence is mixed in this regard. For example, a preliminary study of Canadian bank CEOs found that the bank that had the least formalized strategy process had the best returns over a decade.[29] Others have noted that trendy modern management techniques did not improve US firm performance but improved reputation and legitimacy and increased CEO compensation.[30]

Second, this dominant model also assumes that the organization is considered to be a subject, can act upon the world and "make" the "right" optimal rational strategic choices. As discussed earlier, most strategy texts are structured following the Cartesian lines of analysis–formulation–optimized action.[31] Others argue that strategies often unfold due to intended and unintended actions that cause other strategies to form and are then understood.[32,33] Often, successful random events are coupled with unrelated actors or causes.[34] Thus, successful strategies may be attributed to unrelated and vague activities such as "risk management" and "CEO leadership."

Third, hard data and analysis are relied upon, cognition is used to recognize patterns, and risk management strategies are codified and communicated. Others have argued that soft data and intuition are equally important, but this is largely neglected by the dominant model.[35] Also, the risk management model is assumed to be a top-down activity reserved for senior management. Many organizations do just the opposite.[36] They create loose boundaries, avoid orthodox patterns and use junior managers to create new visions of their futures.[37,38]

Fourth, the quant risk management approach is temporal-centric and USA-centric. Temporal-centric means that the model and its recent incremental variations assume that it is the most advanced and contemporary way of dealing with risk, even though its antecedents are dated.[39,40] Observers have also noted that this model and its texts became nested and sedimented within business schools. The business school, with its quantitative and analytic functional silos, emerged as the dominant design in management education in the USA and remains in that position. Although there is scant academic evidence to suggest that the dominant quant RM model, when used in isolation, is successful, or used in the manner prescribed, business schools outside the USA engage in the mimetic perpetuation of the dominant risk management quant model in order to further teaching at all levels and facilitate consultancy and research. Other descriptive schools have emerged and continue to compete with the traditional prescriptive view of strategy for a share of the minds of managers and academics.[41,42]

Fifth, old ideas are modified incrementally due to this process. As in academe, stasis is maintained in many large organizations by the above "risk management process," and it may simply reaffirm muddling through until crises cause changes to happen in quantum leaps.

An Alternative Approach: Holistic Risk Management

Most risk managers, MBAs and undergraduate students are exposed to the above body of knowledge in numerous courses, often complemented by intensive case analysis and number crunching. Decisive answers are produced from available case facts and figures garnered from simplified self-contained case data and convenient case appendices.

This volume comprises readings that highlight RM failures. Mintzberg has noted that students are overequipped with the tools and techniques of truncated analysis such as the dominant quant risk management model discussed above, and that other reflective, collaborative, worldly and action mindsets are essential for managerial effectiveness.[43]

Exposure to the Holistic Risk Management Model is one way for practitioners and students of risk management to step away from the rule of the tool that is the dominant quant RM model. Although by no means exhaustive, the HRMM and cases contained herein will have risk managers and students reading and thinking in new directions.

This Book: De-freezing and Describing Prescription

This book has underlined that risk means different things to different people for different reasons. The dominant RM quant model outlined above has been treated, along with its implicit assumptions and limitations. It has been noted that the dominant quant RM model is also useful for ceremonial purposes as it creates an illusion of control, yet it may provide little foresight due to its inherent biases.[44,45]

Re-freezing: Prescribing Description

Competing views of risk management have been introduced in the chapters of this volume that challenge the conventional risk management model. I have highlighted the cases that represent interesting and different approaches to risk management in Figure 8.3.

As discussed above, Quadrant 4 in Figure 8.3 represents the case when risk managers do not understand economic and non-economic logics and assign causality to and create sense from observed events.[46,47]

**Risk Governor Understanding of
Non-Economic Logics**

	Quadrant 1	Quadrant 3
High	**Quant-Rational RM** analysis → rules control/ create → optimal events "MARKETS WORK"	**Contrarian RM** events → manipulation/ deviation "GAME THE OTHER BOXES" Cases: Parmalat (ch. 4), UBS and SocGen (ch. 7)
	Quadrant 4	Quadrant 2
Low	**Evolutionary RM** chance and incumbency → suboptimal events "ACCIDENTS HAPPEN" Cases: National Australia Bank (ch. 5) and Gaspesia (ch. 6)	**Institutional RM** social structure → events or inertia "INSTITUTIONS WORK" Case: Canadian Banking (ch. 3)

*Risk Governor
Understanding
of Economic
Logics*

Low   **High**

FIGURE 8.3 The Holistic Risk Management Model (HRMM)

This evolutionary model of strategy would suggest that an organization could be viewed as being the object of random variation within a population. Suboptimal strategies are selected, retained and infused with meaning by chance events and the deeply entrenched orthodoxies, identifications and discourses of societies, organizations, groups and managers.[48,49] Westley et al. call related complex processes "getting to maybe."[50]

As represented by Quadrant 2, institutional RM (in Figure 8.3), the power and structure of the environment may override attempts at foresight by organizational planners. For example, Vit and Graham have noted that the top five Canadian banks enjoyed 85 percent of market share one hundred years ago and continue to do so, even though laws have been changed to permit foreign bank entry.[51] Vit has called the powerful pressures of conformity sedimented within industry and organizational structures "conformist strategy."[52]

An understanding of the dynamics of the four quadrants presented in Figure 8.3 may improve our understanding of risk management since they describe how highly risky situations form, are managed and also in some cases are ignored.

The HRMM shown in Figure 8.3 presents a more holistic route to risk management. Simon has noted that facts are selected, valued and acted upon differently and often suboptimally based upon predispositions that exist in the mind of the manager.[53] Vickers calls this an appreciative system.[54] How and why do common and different risk predispositions emerge? How is it some individuals make connections between seemingly unconnected facts that allow them to create new paradigms and manage radical displacements?[55,56] We do not know enough about where big new disruptive risks come from and how they are induced within complex systems. The development and management of intellect requires an understanding of instrumental know-how and know-what, but it also increasingly means that we must help managers ask more holistic and difficult questions to know why and care why.[57]

This book, among others, has noted that the risky behavior of organizations can be understood by examining different underlying processes that exist to standardize behavior.[58,59,60,61,62] For example, the standardization of work processes and outputs will lead to conformity within the context of a machine organization such as a bank bureaucracy. The standardization of beliefs can lead to predictable behavior by organizations and sadly may provide insight into more extreme forms of ideologically driven action such as terrorism.[63] The standardization of expert skills may lead to proficiency and cognition being codified in expert systems such as those related to medical diagnosis that also have high predictive power. Thus, standardizing and non-standardizing economic and non-economic forces and forms interact and create risky situations when attempting to understand and control risk. This dialogue is represented in Figure 8.3 as the Holistic Risk Management Model (HRMM).

Institutional theory is useful to explain how large organizations behave within a broader context, including business schools. As outlined by the constructs described in Quadrant 2 of Figure 8.3, institutional risk management provides a powerful non-economic explanation of conformity.[64,65,66] A higher level of analysis is also useful as it includes organizations that are interdependent and complex within an organizational field.[67] For example, I have argued that large banks may decouple from economic rationality for years and continue to build legitimacy for questionable actions by relying upon socially nested routines and beliefs. The body of knowledge that is institutional theory may explain the question and risk paradox of "individualistic herding" by practitioners, students and business schools underlined by the discussion above. It may help in answering the question of why large businesses are full of very clever and rational individuals who often teach common recipes that do not work. It might also consider contrarian anomalous organizations, business schools and individuals that intentionally or unintentionally successfully deviate from the pack.[68]

This volume has explored ideas related to contingency, incumbency, social structure and change. Observers have noted that most students of organizations are encouraged to work as individuals throughout their undergraduate and graduate careers, yet organizational life requires an understanding of interdependencies that inhibit and accelerate action.[69] Thus, universities are recruiting and producing students who are very good at getting high grades by memorizing and applying handy analytic models that may be detrimental to the synthesis involved in independent critical thought.[70] Rather than ignoring these invisible forces, an understanding of holistic risk management may lead to more effective forethought, action, change and afterthought.

The HRMM is not bound in time or space. It can be applied to business history and particularly panics, manias and crashes. For example, building upon Minsky's work on the economics of disaster, Kindleberger has suggested that most manias occur due to a displacement that creates three phases: boom-euphoria, mania-bubble and revulsion-crash.[71,72] Although bubbles are easy to spot ex post, the decoupling of economic rationality and its override by social forces that build legitimacy are worthy of attention a priori. Due to their dramatic economic and social impact, the cases in this volume have exposed students of risk management to accounts of various recent risk management failures in the same way that students of geology study earthquakes. This book has dealt with the problem of conformity. It has suggested that the dominant quant model used to teach risk management has many hidden underlying assumptions that build conformity. Also, the quant RM model is ethically empty, as the instrumentality of quant RM can be used for good or nefarious purposes. Further, the dominant RM quant model may or may not work. If we agree with the preceding discussion suggesting that it often may not appreciably improve risk management or foresight, what are we left with? We are left with the understanding of risk as a system of economic, evolutionary, institutional and contrarian processes that explain risk. When understood, I argue here that they can also be used to mitigate risk and promote critical thought and action. The chapters of this text have outlined that the problem of conformity is reinforced at many levels of analysis, and that both economic and social logics must be considered.

We do not know precisely why some managers and leaders follow blindly and others do not.[73] Our understanding of patterns in conformist managerial behavior is not complete, and nor is unorthodox or contrarian managerial behavior fully understood. Morison has observed that the limited identification of individuals with in-groups as well as out-groups may help explain both.[74] Tremendous pressure to conform also exists within organizations, new and old, small and large. Strong organizational ideologies create common values that may override atomistic value-maximizing economic behavior. Social forces, orthodoxies and embedded organizational algorithms may create taken-for-granted cognitive routines that may not require critical questioning or contrarian behavior. Although we may not understand or be able to fully foresee the impact of displacements on managers, organizations, organizational fields and economic booms and busts, an understanding of the dynamics of conformity and non-conformity using the HRMM allows us to be aware of pressures that close down independent thought and action. Contrarianism begins with this understanding. In order to understand how being different can be advantageous or disadvantageous, it is necessary to understand the dynamics of conformity.

This book has opened up other problems and risk topics that have major managerial and human relevance. Further research should be devoted to contrarian organizations such as non-owned organizations and their role in our world. Many organizations such as universities and NGOs are not accountable to shareholders. Social purpose and social innovation may eclipse the maximization of free cash flow. Beyond factory-type organizations that may lend themselves to bureaucracy and quant risk managing, other organizational forms such as networks, cooperatives and micro-credit lending agencies represent interesting alternative forms of action and risk. Risk management models related to managing risk within these organizations also need to be explored.[75] Observers have noted that management and business teaching and research applications cater to less than a billion human beings within developed nations.[76] "Bottom of the pyramid" approaches to risk management that address risks related to the other five or six billion inhabitants of this planet represent another promising contrarian contribution to risk management.

As noted, SWOT analyses together with risk management formulation and implementation are instrumental and sterile. They do not deal with ethical issues and social questions such as the dangers and risks of technological advancement, which may have a major impact upon managers and society. For example, Joy has noted that nuclear, biological and chemical weapons of mass destruction (WMD) were in the past largely controlled by governments, yet new self-replicating technologies such as genomics, nano-technology and robotics are potentially open to abuse by many individuals and groups.[77] This risk must also be considered and managed. In the race for material gain, growth and commercialization, willful or accidental mass replication could have serious negative consequences. These risks need to be contemplated and students and managers need to think about personal moral dilemmas and risk. While significant attention is given to governance at a top management and board level using reductionist checklists, effective thought, understanding and responsibility for potentially revolutionary change must occur at an individual level.

For example, Bird and Shirwin have noted that the intended and unintended consequences of the creation of the nuclear bomb were not foreseen by J. Robert Oppenheimer and his colleagues.[78] Few policy researchers write about big problems and big risks. An exception is Allison, who ends on a cautiously optimistic note regarding the threat and prevention of nuclear terrorism.[79]

This brief volume has argued that a well-worn dominant quant risk management model is still pervasive and present in texts and the practice and teaching of risk management. We may foresee with some certainty that this model will continue to contribute to the problem of conformity in risk management practice, education and research.

This book and the Holistic Risk Management Model (HRMM) presented herein has also suggested several promising alternative views of risk management. A first step to improving our understanding of risk management is to continue to follow new lines of thinking about risk. Together, these multiple and holistic ways of viewing risk should have a much greater impact on understanding the risk IN risk management.

Notes

1 The Problem of Conformity in Financial Organizations

1　Lounsbury, M. and Hirsch, P. (2010). Markets on Trial: Toward a Policy-Oriented Economic Sociology. In M. Lounsbury and P. Hirsch (eds.) *Markets on Trial: The Economic Sociology of the U.S. Financial Crisis*, Research in the Sociology of Organizations 30. Bingley: Emerald.

2　United States of America, Financial Crisis Inquiry Commission (2011). *The Financial Crisis Inquiry Report*, commissioned by Angelides, P., Thomas, B., Born, B., Murren, H.H., Graham, B. et al. (Washington: U.S. Government Printing Office).

3　Vit, G. (2007). The Multiple Logics of Conformity and Contrarianism: The Problem with Investment Banks and Bankers. *Journal of Management Inquiry*, 16 (3), 217–226.

4　Smith, A. (1776). *An Inquiry into the Nature and Causes of the Wealth of Nations.* London: Methuen & Co., Ltd.

5　Galbraith, J.K. (2004). *The Economics of Innocent Fraud.* New York: Houghton Mifflin Company.

6　Kindleberger, C. (1978). *Manias, Panics and Crashes: A History of Financial Crises.* New York: Basic Books.

7　Vit, pp. 217–226.

8　United States of America, Financial Crisis Inquiry Commission, p. 132.

9　Financial Crisis Inquiry Report (2011). *Final Report of the National Commission on the Causes of the Financial and Economic Crisis in the United States.* New York: US Government Printing Office.

10　Ibid, p. 121.

11　Ibid.

12　Gimpl, M. and Dakin, S. (1984). Management and Magic. *California Management Review*, 27 (1), 125–136.

13 Galbraith.

14 Asquith, P., Mullins, J., and Wolff, E.D. (1989). Original Issue High Yield Bonds: Aging Analyses of Defaults, Exchanges, and Calls. *Journal of Finance*, 44 (September), 923–952.

2 The Holistic Risk Management Model (HRMM)

1 Clegg, S., Carter, C., and Kornberger, M. (2004). Get up, I Feel Like Being a Strategy Machine. *European Management Review*, 1 (1), 21–28.

2 Vit, G. (2009). Foreseeing the Problem of Conformity in Strategy Teaching, Research and Practice. In B. MacKay and L. Constanza (eds.) *The Handbook of Research on Strategy and Foresight*. Northampton, MA: Edward Elgar Publishing Limited, 518–527.

3 For example, see International Organization for Standardization (2009). *ISO 31000: 2009: Risk Management Principles and Guidelines*. Geneva: International Organization for Standardization.

4 Vit, G. (2006). Organizational Conformity and Contrarianism: Regular Irregular Trading at National Australia Bank. *Corporate Governance*, 6 (2), 203–214.

5 Vit, G. (2009).

6 Vit, G. and Graham, J. (1997). Canada Changes Foreign Bank Laws. *Butterworth's Journal of International Banking and Financial Law*, September, 363–368.

7 Other competing views and ex post 2008 crisis accounts of the crisis hail the fact that Canadian banks ring fence and limit total exposures, and only do what they understand (CEO's comments, TD annual report, 2010), which would be a Quadrant 1 of Figure 2.1 argument.

8 Westley, F. and Bird, F. (1990). The Sociology of Organizational Commitment: A Comparative Review of Classical Theories. Working Paper, McGill Univeristy.

9 Gould, S.J. (1987). The Panda's Thumb of Technology. *Natural History*, 96 (1), 16–23.

10 Asquith, P., Mullins, J., and Wolff, E.D. (1989). Original Issue High Yield Bonds: Aging Analyses of Defaults, Exchanges, and Calls. *Journal of Finance*, 44, 923–952.

11 Palmer, D. and Maher, M.W. (2010). A Normal Accident Analysis of the Mortgage Meltdown. In M. Lounsbury and P. Hirsch (eds.) *Markets on Trial: The Economic Sociology of the U.S. Financial Crisis*, Research in the Sociology of Organizations 30. Bingley: Emerald.

12 Perrow, C. (2010). The Meltdown Was Not an Accident. In M. Lounsbury and P. Hirsch (eds.) *Markets on Trial: The Economic Sociology of the U.S. Financial Crisis*, Research in the Sociology of Organizations 30. Bingley: Emerald, 309–330.

13 Thompson, J. (1967). *Organizations in Action: Social Science Bases of Administrative Theory*. London: Transaction Publishers.

14 Vickers, G. (1965). *The Art of Judgment: A Study of Policy Making*. London: Chapman and Hall.

15 Vit, G. (2007). The Multiple Logics of Conformity and Contrarianism: The Problem with Investment Banks and Bankers. *Journal of Management Inquiry*, 16 (3), 217–226.
16 Vit, G. (2009).
17 Morison, E. (1966). Gunfire at Sea: A Case Study of Innovation. In E. Morison (ed.) *Men, Machines and Modern Times*. Cambridge, MA: MIT Press, 17–44.
18 Elsbach, K. (1999). An Expanded Model of Organizational Identification. In R. Sutton and B.M. Staw (eds.) *Research in Organizational Behaviour*, 21. London: JAI Press, 163–199.

3 Institutional Risk Management: Case 1, The Canadian Banking Paradigm

1 Vit, G. (1996). Financial Services Industry Mismanagement: Institutionalization and Conformist Strategy. *International Journal of Service Industry Management*, 7 (3), 6–16.
2 DiMaggio, P. and Powell, W. (1991). *The New Institutionalism in Organizational Analysis*. Chicago, IL: University of Chicago Press.
3 Ibid., p. 150.
4 Allison, G. (1971). *The Essence of Decision: Explaining the Cuban Missile Crisis*. London: Little Brown & Co.
5 Brunsson, N. (1982). The Irrationality of Action and Action Rationality: Decisions, Ideologies and Organizational Actions. *Journal of Management Studies*, 19 (1), 29–44.
6 Butler, R. (1991). *Designing Organizations: A Decision-Making Perspective*. London: Routledge.
7 Gimpl, M. and Dakin, S. (1984). Management and Magic. *California Management Review*, 27 (1), 125–136.
8 Mintzberg, H. (1991). The Effective Organization: Forces and Forms. *Sloan Management Review*, 32 (2), 57–67.
9 Pascale, R. (1984). Perspectives on Strategy: The Real Story behind Honda's Success. *California Management Review*, 26 (3), 47–72.
10 Pascale, R. (1990). *Managing on the Edge: How the Smartest Companies Use Conflict to Stay Ahead*. New York: Simon & Schuster.
11 Seegar, J. (1984). Research Notes and Communication: Reversing the Images of BCG's Growth/Share Matrix. *Strategic Management Journal*, 5, 93–97.
12 Vit, G. (1993). Canadian Bank Strategy: The CEO's Perspective. *CETAI Cahier de Recherche*, 93–18, Ecole des Hautes Etudes Commerciale, Montreal, Canada.
13 Pettigrew, A. (1992). The Character and Significance of Strategy Process Research. *Strategic Management Journal*, 13, 5–16.
14 Pfeffer, J. (1993). Barriers to the Advancement of Organizational Science: Paradigm Development as a Dependent Variable. *Academy of Management Review*, 18 (4), 599–620.
15 Spender, J. (1993). Some Frontier Activities around Strategy Theorizing. *Journal of Management Studies*, 30 (1), 11–29.

16 Alvesson, M. (1991). Organizational Symbolism and Ideology. *Journal of Management Studies*, 28 (3), 207–225.

17 Covaleski, M. and Dirsmith, M. (1988). An Institutional Perspective on the Rise, Social Transformation, and Fall of a University Budget Category. *Administrative Science Quarterly*, 13 (4), 562–587.

18 Ibid., p. 585.

19 Zucker, L. (1987). Institutional Theories of Organization. *Annual Review of Sociology*, 13, 443–464.

20 Scott, W. (1995). *Institutions and Organizations*. London: Sage Publications.

21 Thompson, J. (1967). *Organizations in Action: Social Science Bases of Administrative Theory*. New York: McGraw-Hill Book Company.

22 Oliver, C. (1991). Strategic Responses to Organizational Processes. *Academy of Management Review*, 16 (1), 145–179.

23 Pfeffer, J. (1982). *Organizations and Organization Theory*. London: Pitman.

24 Pfeffer, J. and Salancik, G. (1978). *The External Control of Organizations: A Resource Dependence Perspective*. New York: Harper & Row.

25 Covalski and Dirsmith.

26 Thompson.

27 Meyer, J. and Rowan, B. (1977). Institutionalized Organizations: Formal Structures as Myth and Ceremony. *American Journal of Sociology*, 83 (2), 340–363.

28 Meyer, J., Rowan, B., Deal, T. and Scott, W. (1983). *Organizational Environments: Ritual and Rationality*. London: Sage Publications.

29 DiMaggio, P. and Powell, M. (1983). The Iron Cage Revisited: Institutional Isomorphism and Collective Rationality in Organizational Fields. *American Sociological Review*, 48 (2), 147–160.

30 Zucker.

31 Darroch, J. and Litvach, A. (1991). Canadian Banks: Strategic Initiatives. *Business Quarterly*, Autumn.

32 Baker, P.L. (1987). Banking Transformed: Women's Work and Technological Change in a Canadian Bank. Unpublished PhD thesis, University of Toronto, Canada.

33 Bank of Canada (1983). *Bank of Canada Review*. Ottawa: Bank of Canada.

34 Darroch, J. (1990). Canadian Bank Strategy. Unpublished PhD thesis, York University, Canada.

35 Ibid., p. 6.

36 Ibid., p. 11.

37 MacIntosh, R. (1991). *Different Drummers: Banking and Politics in Canada*. Toronto: Macmillan of Canada.

38 Ibid., p. 113.

39 Ibid., p. 118.

40 Bank of Canada.

41 Ibid., p. 3.

42 MacIntosh.

43 Ibid., p. 164.

44 Bank of Canada (1987). Text of a speech given by John W. Crow, Governor of the Bank of Canada, to the 71st Annual Meeting of the Investment Dealers' Association of Canada, Ottawa, June 9.

45 DiMaggio and Powell.

46 Nowzad, B. (1990). Lessons of the Debt Debacle. *Finance and Development*, 27 (March), 9–13.

47 DiMaggio and Powell.

48 Meyer, J. and Rowan, B. (1977). Institutional Organizations: Formal Structure as Myth and Ceremony. *American Journal of Sociology*, 83 (2), 340–363.

49 Alvesson.

50 Cray, D. and Colignon, R. (1980). Critical Organizations. *Organizational Studies*, 1 (4), 349–365.

51 Westley, F. and Bird, F. (1990). The Sociology of Organizational Commitment: A Comparative Review of Classical Theories. Working Paper, McGill Univeristy.

52 Hurst, D. (1986). Why Strategic Management Is Bankrupt. *Organizational Dynamics*, 15 (2), 5–27.

53 Mintzberg, H. (1994). The Fall and Rise of Strategic Planning. *Harvard Business Review*, 72, Jan./Feb.

54 Simon, H. (1945). *Administrative Behavior*. New York: Macmillan.

55 Vickers, G. (1965). *The Art of Judgment: A Study of Policy Making*. London: Chapman and Hall.

56 Geertz, R. (1973). *Notes on the Balinese Cockfight in the Interpretation of Cultures*. New York: Basic Books.

57 Hofstede, G. (1990). Motivation, Leadership, and Organizations: Do American Theories Apply Abroad? *Organizational Dynamics*, 19 (Summer).

58 Jaeger, A. and Kanungo, R. (1990). Management in Developing Countries. *Strategic Management Journal*, 9, 31–41.

59 Marsden, D. (1991). Indigenous Management. *Journal of Human Resource Management*, 2 (1).

60 Mintzberg (1991).

61 Schein, E. (1983). The Role of the Founder in Creating Organizational Culture. *Organizational Dynamics*, 12 (1), 13–28.

62 Srinivas, N. (1992). Indigenous Management. *CETAI Cahier de Recherche*, 92–16, Ecole des Hautes Etudes Commerciales, Montreal, Canada.

63 Westley and Bird.

64 Mintzberg, H. (1990). Strategy Formation: Schools of Thought. In J. Fredrickson (ed.) *Perspectives on Strategic Management*. New York: Harper Business.

4 Contrarian Risk Management and Fraud: Case 2, The Parmalat Fraud

1 "The Breaking the Frame Award" for best *Journal of Management Inquiry* article in 2007.

2 Goldstone, J. (Producer) and Jones, T. (Director) (1979). *Monty Python's Life of Brian*. United Kingdom: Cinema International Corporation.

3 Ibid.

4 Parmalat S.p.A. Sede (2003). *Parmalat*. Retrieved from http://www.parmalat.com/en/.

5 Sylvers, E. (2005). Parmalat Trial in Milan Nets 11 Convictions. *International Herald Tribune*, June 29.

6 Dobson, W. (2004). Parmalat's Babcock Institute Discussion Paper No. 2004-4. Madison, WI: The Babcock Institute for International Dairy Research and Development.

7 Vit, G. (2006). Organizational Conformity and Contrarianism: Regular Irregular Trading at National Australia Bank. *Corporate Governance*, 6 (2), 203–214.

8 Smith, M. (2005). The Paramalat Syndrome. *SF Weekly*, January 12.

9 Covaleski, M. and Dirsmith, M. (1988). An Institutional Perspective on the Rise, Social Transformation and Fall of a University Budget Category. *Administrative Science Quarterly*, 13 (4), 562–587.

10 Dobson.

11 Barigazzi, J. (2004). Parmalat's Ex-finance Chief Blames Boss. *Globe and Mail*, June 1.

12 Michaels, A. (2004). Court Grants Parmalat Claims. *Financial Times*, Dec. 17.

13 Vit, G. (1996). Financial Services Industry Mismanagement: Institutionalization and Conformist Strategy. *International Journal of Service Industry Management*, 7 (3), 6–16.

14 Gould, S. (1987). The Panda's Thumb of Technology. *Natural History*, 96 (1), 16–23.

15 Merton, R.C. (1973). Theory of Rational Option Pricing. *Bell Journal of Economics and Management Science*, 4, 141–183.

16 Merton, R.K. (1938). Social Structure and Anomie. *American Sociological Review*, 3 (5), 672–682.

17 Vit (1996).

18 Shapira, Z. and Berndt, D.J. (1997). Managing Grand Scale Construction Projects: A Risk-Taking Perspective. *Research in Organizational Behaviour*, 19, 303–360.

19 Zajac, E. and Westphal, J. (2004). The Social Construction of Market Value: Institutionalization and Learning Perspectives on Stock Market Reactions. *American Sociological Review*, 69 (3), 433–457.

20 Lounsbury, M. (2007). The Tale of Two Cities: Competing Logics and Practice Variation in the Professionalizing of Mutual Funds' Forthcoming. *Academy of Management Journal*, 50 (2), 289–307.

21 Vit (2006).

22 Ibid.

23 Merton, R.K. (1936). The Unanticipated Consequences of Purposive Social Action. *American Sociological Review*, 1 (6), 894–904.

24 Thompson, J. and Tudon, A. (1959). Strategies, Structure, and Processes of

Organizational Decision. In J. Thompson, P.B. Iammond, R.W. Hawkes and A. Tudon (eds.) *Comparative Studies in Administration.* Pittsburgh, PA: University of Pittsburgh Press.

25 Vickers, G. (1965). *The Art of Judgment: A Study of Policy Making.* London: Chapman and Hall.

26 Feldman, M. and Pentland, B. (2003). Reconceptualizing Organizational Routines as a Source of Flexibility and Change. *Administrative Science Quarterly,* 48 (1), 94–118.

27 Vickers.

28 Simon, H. (1945). *Administrative Behavior.* New York: Macmillan.

29 Clegg, S., Carter, C., and Kornberger, M. (2004). Get up, I Feel Like Being a Strategy Machine. *European Management Review,* 1 (1), 21–28.

30 Brealey, R. (1985). *An Introduction to Risk and Return.* London: Blackwell.

31 DiMaggio, P. and Powell, M. (1983). The Iron Cage Revisited: Institutional Isomorphism and Collective Rationality in Organizational Fields. *American Sociological Review,* 48 (2), 147–160.

32 Meyer, J. and Rowan, B. (1977). Institutionalized Organizations: Formal Structures as Myth and Ceremony. *American Journal of Sociology,* 83 (2), 340–363.

33 Thompson, J. (1967). *Organizations in Action: Social Science Bases of Administrative Theory.* London: Transaction Publishers.

34 Phillips, N., Lawrence, T.B., and Hardy, C. (2004). Discourse and Institutions. *Academy of Management Review,* 29, 635–652.

35 *Oxford Dictionary of English,* 2nd ed. (2005). Oxford: Oxford University Press.

36 Ibid.

37 Ibid.

38 DiMaggio and Powell.

39 Scott, W. (1995). *Institutions and Organizations.* London: Sage Publications.

40 Holm, P. (1995). The Dynamics of Institutionalization: Transformation Processes in Norwegian Fisheries. *Administrative Science Quarterly,* 40 (3), 398–422.

41 Vit (2006).

42 Vit (1996).

43 Mintzberg, H. (1991). The Effective Organization: Forces and Forms. *Sloan Management Review,* 32 (2), 57–67.

44 Greenwood, R. and Hinings, C. (1988). Design Archetypes, Tracks and the Dynamics of Strategic Change. *Organization Studies,* 9 (3), 293–316.

45 Mintzberg, H. (1979). *The Structuring of Organizations: A Synthesis of the Research.* Englewood Cliffs, NJ: Prentice Hall.

46 Mintzberg, H. (1983). *Structure in Fives: Designing Effective Organizations.* Englewood Cliffs, NJ: Prentice Hall.

47 Mintzberg (1991).

48 Thompson (1967).

49 Mintzberg (1979).

50 Miller, D. (1987). The Genesis of Configuration. *The Academy of Management Review,* 12 (4), 686–701.

51 Maguire, S. (2003). The Co-evolution of Technology and Discourse: A Study of Substitution Processes for the Insecticide DDT. *Organization Studies*, 25(1), 113–134.

52 Selznick, P. (1957). *Leadership in Administration: A Sociological Interpretation*. London: Harper & Row.

53 Zald, M. and Denton, P. (1963). From Evangelism to General Service: The Transformation of the YMCA. *Administrative Science Quarterly*, 8 (2), 214–234.

54 Suddaby, R. and Greenwood, R. (2005). Rhetorical Strategies of Legitimacy. *Administrative Science Quarterly*, 50 (1), 35–67.

55 Morison, E. (1966). Gunfire at Sea: A Case Study of Innovation. In E. Morison (ed.) *Men, Machines and Modern Times*. Cambridge, MA: MIT Press, 17–44.

56 Abrahamson, E. and Fairchild, G. (1999). Management Fashion: Lifecycles, Triggers, and Collective Learning Processes. *Administrative Science Quarterly*, 44 (4), 708–740.

57 Staw, B. and Epstein, L. (2000). What Bandwagons Bring: Effects of Popular Management Techniques on Corporate Performance, Reputation, and CEO Pay. *Administrative Science Quarterly*, 45 (3), 523–556.

58 Vickers.

59 Ferrari, U., Brocklehurst, C., and Wright, A. (2002). Tulips, Railways and Telecom. *UBS Warburg Global Equity Research*, 1–41.

60 MacKay, C. (1914). *Memoirs of Extraordinary Popular Delusions and the Madness of Crowds*, reprinted ed. (1932). Boston: L.C. Page Co.

61 Kondratieff, N.D. and Stolper, W.F. (1935). The Long Waves in Economic Life. *Review of Economic Statistics*, 17 (6), 105–115.

62 Minsky, H.P. (1972). Financial Stability Revisited: The Economics of Disaster. *Board of Governors of the Federal Reserve System, Reappraisal of the Federal Reserve Discount Mechanism*, 3, 95–136.

63 Kindleberger, C. (1978). *Manias, Panics and Crashes: A History of Financial Crises*. New York: Basic Books.

64 Anderson, P. and Tushman, M. (1991). Managing through Cycles of Technological Change. *Research Technology Management*, 34 (3), 26.

65 Strebel, P. (1992). *Breakpoints: How Managers Exploit Radical Business Change*. New York: Harvard Business Press.

66 Christensen, C., Craig, T., and Hart, S. (2001). The Great Disruption. *Foreign Affairs*, 80 (2), 80–95.

67 Kindleberger.

68 Vickers.

69 Abolafia, M. and Kilduff, M. (1988). Enacting Market Crisis: The Social Construction of a Speculative Bubble. *Administrative Science Quarterly*, 33 (2), 177–193.

70 Mello, A., Attari, M. and Ruckes, M. (2003). Arbitraging Arbitrageurs. *Journal of Finance*, 60 (5), 2471–2511.

71 Aldrich, H. and Ruef, M. (1999). *Organizations Evolving*. Thousand Oaks, CA: Sage Publications.

72 Oliver, C. (1992). The Antecedents of Deinstitutionalization. *Organization Studies*, 13 (4), 563–588.

73 Lawrence, T., Winn, M., and Jennings, P. (2001). The Temporal Dynamics of Institutionalization. *Academy of Management Review*, 26 (4), 624–645.

5 Evolutionary Risk Management: Case 3, The National Australia Bank Fraud

1 Galbraith, J. (2004). *The Economics of Innocent Fraud: Truth for Our Time*. New York: Houghton Mufflin Books, p. 39.

2 Australian Prudential Regulation Authority (2004). *Report into Irregular Currency Options Trading at the National Australia Bank*. Sydney: Commonwealth of Australia, p. 5.

3 National Australia Bank (n.d.). Retrieved from http://www.nab.com.au/.

4 Thompson, J. and Tudon, A. (1959). Strategies, Structure, and Processes of Organizational Decision. In J. Thompson, P.B. Iammond, R.W. Hawkes, and A. Tudon (eds.) *Comparative Studies in Administration*. Pittsburgh., PA: University of Pittsburgh Press.

5 Nelson, R. (1991). How Do Firms Differ and Why Does It Matter? *Strategic Management Journal*, 12 (2), 61–74.

6 Australian Prudential Regulation Authority, p. 20.

7 Thompson, J. (1967). *Organizations in Action: Social Science Bases of Administrative Theory*. New York: McGraw-Hill Book Company.

8 Fayol, H. (1916). *General and Industrial Management*. New York: Pitman.

9 Andrews, K. (1965). *The Concept of Corporate Strategy*. Homewood, IL: Dow Jones Irwin.

10 Simon, H. (1945). *Adminstrative Behavior*. New York: The Free Press.

11 Vickers, G. (1965). *The Art of Judgment: A Study of Policy Making*. London: Chapman and Hall.

12 Vit, G. (1996). Financial Services Industry Mismanagement: Institutionalization and Conformist Strategy. *International Journal of Service Industry Management*, 7 (3), 6–16.

13 DiMaggio, P. and Powell, M. (1983). The Iron Cage Revisited: Institutional Isomorphism and Collective Rationality in Organizational Fields. *American Sociological Review*, 48 (2), 147–160.

14 Scott, W. (1995). *Institutions and Organizations*. London: Sage Publications.

15 Kindleberger, C. (1978). *Manias, Panics and Crashes: A History of Financial Crises*. New York: Basic Books.

16 Simon, H. (1979). Rational Decision Making in Business Organizations. *American Economic Review*, 69 (4), 495–513.

17 Mintzberg, H. (1983). *Structure in Fives: Designing Effective Organizations*. Englewood Cliffs, NJ: Prentice Hall.

18 Greenwood, R. and Hinings, C. (1988). Organizational Design Types, Tracks and the Dynamics of Strategic Change. *Organization Studies*, 9 (3), 293–316.

19 Miller, D. (1987). The Genesis of Configuration. *Academy of Management Review*, 12 (4), 686–701.

20 Miller, D. (1993). The Architecture of Simplicity. *Academy of Management Review*, 18 (1), 116–138.

21 Miller, D. (1996). Configurations Revisited. *Strategic Management Journal*, 17 (7), 505–512.

22 Thompson (1967).

23 Meyer, J. and Rowan, B. (1977). Institutionalized Organizations: Formal Structures as Myth and Ceremony. *American Journal of Sociology*, 83 (2), 340–363.

24 DiMaggio and Powell.

25 Australian Prudential Regulation Authority, p. 21.

26 Achbar, M. and Wintonick, P. (1992). *Manufacturing Consent: Noam Chomsky and the Media*, documentary film, National Film Board of Canada, Montreal.

27 Merton, R.K. (1936). The Unanticipated Consequences of Purposive Social Action. *American Sociological Review*, 1 (6), 894–904.

28 Mintzberg, H. (1979). *The Structuring of Organizations: A Synthesis of the Research*. Englewood Cliffs, NJ: Prentice Hall.

29 Miller (1993).

30 Elsbach, K. (1999). An Expanded Model of Organizational Identification. In B.M. Staw and R.I. Sutton (eds.) *Research in Organizational Behaviour*, 21, pp. 163–200.

31 Ashforth, B.E. and Mael, F. (1989). Social Identity Theory and the Organization. *Academy of Management Review*, 14 (1), 20–39.

32 Zald, M. and Denton, P. (1963). From Evangelism to General Service: The Transformation of the YMCA. *Administrative Science Quarterly*, 8 (2), 214–234.

33 Selznick, P. (1957). *Leadership in Administration: A Sociological Interpretation*. London: Harper & Row.

34 Mintzberg (1983).

35 Westley, F. and Bird, F. (1990). The Sociology of Organizational Commitment: A Comparative Review of Classical Theories. Working Paper, McGill University.

36 Mortensen, M. and Hinds, P. (2002). Fuzzy Teams: Boundary Disagreement in Distributed and Collocated Teams. In P. Hinds and S. Kiesler (eds.) *Distributed Work*. Cambridge, MA: MIT Press, pp. 281–308.

37 Galbraith.

38 Australian Prudential Regulation Authority, p. 72.

39 Bullen, D. (2004). *Fake: My Life as a Rogue Trader*. Mississauga: Wiley, pp. 84–85.

40 Defined as the tools used to measure and track risk.

41 Defined as coercive and mimetic conformist forces.

42 Defined as cultural conformist coordinating mechanisms such as the standardization of norms.

43 Merton.

44 Holm, P. (1995). The Dynamics of Institutionalization: Transformation Processes in Norwegian Fisheries. *Administrative Science Quarterly*, 40 (30), 398–422.

45 Greenwood, R. and Hinings, C. (1993). Understanding Strategic Change: The Contribution of Archetypes. *Academy of Management Journal*, 36 (5), 1052–1081.

46 Vickers.

47 Simon, H. (1945). *Administrative Behaviour*. New York: Macmillan.

48 Vickers, p. 67.
49 Merton.
50 Mintzberg, H. and Waters, J. (1985). Of Strategies, Deliberate and Emergent. *Strategic Management Journal*, 6 (3), 257–272.
51 Mintzberg, H. (1991). The Effective Organization: Forces and Forms. *Sloan Management Review*, 32 (2), 57–67.
52 Merton, R.K. (1938). Social Structure and Anomie. *American Sociological Review*, 3 (5), 672–682.
53 Mintzberg (1991).
54 Greenwood and Hinings (1993).
55 Miller (1996).

6 Evolutionary Risk Management: Case 4, The Gaspesia Project Fiasco

1 Vit, G. (1996). Financial Services Industry Mismanagement: Institutionalization and Conformist Strategy. *International Journal of Service Industry Management*, 7 (3), 6–16.
2 Lesage, R. (2005). Rapport d'enquête sur les dépassements de coûts et de délais du chantier de la Société Papiers Gaspésia de Chandler / Commission d'enquête sur la Société Papiers Gaspésia. Québec: Commission d'enquête sur la Société Papiers Gaspésia. Quebec, Canada.
3 Staw, B.M. (1981). The Escalation of Commitment to a Course of Action. *Academy of Management Review*, 6 (4), 577–587.
4 Ross, J. and Staw, B. (1993). Organizational Escalation and Exit: Lessons from the Shoreham Nuclear Power Plant. *Academy of Management Journal*, 36 (4), 701–732.
5 Keil, M. (1995). Pulling the Plug: Software Project Management and the Problem of Project Escalation. *MIS Quarterly*, 19 (4), 421–447.
6 McNamara, G., Moon, H., and Bronmiley, P. (2002). Banking on Commitment: Intended and Unintended Consequences of an Organization's Attempt to Attenuate Escalation of Commitment. *Academy of Management Journal*, 45 (2), 443–452.
7 Golden-Biddle, K. and Hayagreeva, R. (1997). Breaches in the Boardroom: Organizational Identity and Conflicts of Commitment in a Non-profit Organization. *Organization Science*, 8 (6), 593–611.
8 Miller, C., Cardinal, L., and Glick, W. (1997). Retrospective Reports in Organizational Research. *Academy of Management Journal*, 40 (1), 189–204.
9 Ocasio, W. (1997). Towards an Attention Based View of the Firm. *Strategic Management Journal*, 18 (1), 187–206.
10 Ross and Staw.
11 Shapira, Z. and Berndt, D. (1997). Managing Grand Scale Construction Projects: A Risk-Taking Perspective. *Research in Organizational Behaviour*, 19, 303–360.
12 Ibid.

13 Vit, G. (2006). Organizational Conformity and Contrarianism: Regular Irregular Trading at National Australia Bank. *Corporate Governance*, 6(2), 203–214.

14 Vit, G. (2007). The Multiple Logics of Conformity and Contrarianism: The Problem with Investment Banks and Bankers. *Journal of Management Inquiry*, 16 (3), 217–226.

15 Martinet, A. (1999). La lecture stratégique du diagnostic global. In A. Marion (ed.) *Le diagnostic d'entreprise: Méthode et processus*. Paris: Economica.

16 Merton, R.K. (1936). The Unanticipated Consequences of Purposive Social Action. *American Sociological Review*, 1 (6), 894–904.

17 Thompson, J. and Tudon, A. (1959). Strategies, Structure, and Processes of Organizational Decision. In J. Thompson, P.B. Iammond, R.W. Hawkes, and A. Tudon (eds.) *Comparative Studies in Administration*. Pittsburgh, PA: Universtiy of Pittsburgh Press.

18 Vickers, G. (1965). *The Art of Judgment: A Study of Policy Making*. London: Chapman and Hall.

19 Martinet.

20 Lounsbury, M. (2007). The Tale of Two Cities: Competing Logics and Practice Variation in the Professionalizing of Mutual Funds' Forthcoming. *Academy of Management Journal*, 50 (2), 289–307.

21 Lesage.

22 Readers may wish to consult the original French language report: see Lesage.

23 Shapira and Berndt.

24 Simon, H. (1945). *Adminstrative Behavior*. New York: The Free Press.

25 Miller et al.

26 Lesage, p. 332.

27 Vit (2006).

28 Vit (2007).

29 Martinet.

30 Thompson, J. (1967). *Organizations in Action: Social Science Bases of Administrative Theory*. London: Transaction Publishers.

31 Mintzberg, H. (1983). *Structure in Fives: Designing Effective Organizations*. Englewood Cliffs, NJ: Prentice Hall.

32 Thompson (1967).

33 Vit (1996).

34 Lesage.

35 Ibid., p. 56.

36 Ibid., p. 178.

37 Tembec, Inc. (2000). Tembec Financial Report 2000, p. 2.

38 Lesage, p. 182.

39 Lesage.

40 Ibid.

41 Miller, R. and Lessard, D. (2000). *The Strategic Management of Large Engineering Projects*. Cambridge, MA: MIT.

42 Lesage, p. 29.

43 Ibid., p. 259.

44 Ramanujam, R. and Goodman, P. (2003). Latent Errors and Adverse Organizational Consequences: A Conceptualization. *Journal of Organizational Behaviour*, 24 (7), 815–836.

45 Vit (2006).

46 Vit (2007).

47 Simon, H. (1979). Rational Decision Making in Business Organizations. *American Economic Review*, 69 (4), 495–513.

48 Fédération des travailleurs du Québec (n.d.). Retrieved from http://ftq.qc.ca/.

49 DiMaggio, P. and Powell, M. (1983). The Iron Cage Revisited: Institutional Isomorphism and Collective Rationality in Organizational Fields. *American Sociological Review*, 48 (2), 147–160.

50 Lesage.

51 Ibid., p. 210.

52 Ibid., p. 248.

53 Shapira and Berndt.

54 Lesage, p. 171.

55 I have used the terms "judicious" and "contrarian" interchangeably when referring to the HRMM in my work. Contrarian is more encompassing as it includes both positive and negative applications of the model.

7 Contrarian Risk Management: Case 5, The UBS Sub-prime Meltdown and Case 6, The Société Générale Fraud

1 KPMG (2008). *Letter of Substantiation in Report to Shareholders on UBS Writedowns.* Zurich.

2 It is also based upon a November 17, 2008, UBS Compensation Report, UBS's 20F filing to the SEC and its amended versions (SEC 2008 and 2009), other UBS financial filings with regulators (UBS 2008a, UBS 2009a) and interviews with market participants.

3 This chapter has also used a detailed SocGen-commissioned PricewaterhouseCoopers external diagnostic review report that was made public on May 23, 2008. It is interesting to note that comments and reports from SocGen's 2007 statutory auditors, Ernst & Young and Deloitte, which gave a clean bill of health regarding internal control procedures on p. 99 of SocGen's 2007 registration report, are conspicuously absent from available data.

4 Subsequent triangulation from interviews, primary and secondary data, external accountants, regulators, competitors, bank officials and other informants that continued after this text was written supports its conclusions.

5 Miller, C., Cardinal, L., and Glick, W. (1997). Retrospective Reports in Organizational Research: A Reexamination of Recent Evidence. *Academy of Management Journal*, 40 (1), 189–204.

6 A 3 percent fee on assets and 30 percent of profit, according to Bloomberg 2007.

7   Note "revenue gaps" not "risk" gaps.

8   UBS (2008a,b). *Shareholder Report on UBS's Writedowns*. Zurich.

9   Ibid., p. 13.

10 UBS suffered more trading losses in London in 2011 when a trader was accused of fraud that resulted in over US$1.5 billion in losses.

11 Société Générale (2007a,b). 2007 Registration Document. Paris: Tour Société Générale, 125–151.

12 Société Générale (2008a,b). General Inspection Department: Mission Green Summary Report. Paris: Tour Société Générale.

13 Vit, G. (2007). The Multiple Logics of Conformity and Contrarianism: The Problem with Investment Banks and Bankers. *Journal of Management Inquiry*, 16 (3), 217–226.

14 UBS (2008a,b), p. 9.

15 Société Générale (2008a,b).

16 Ibid., p. 18.

17 PricewaterhouseCoopers (2008). Société Générale: Summary of PwC Diagnostic Review and Analysis of the Action Plan. Paris, p. 6.

18 Ibid.

19 Schwartz, N. and Bennhold, K. (2008). In France, the Heads No Longer Roll. *New York Times*, February 17.

20 Gould, S.J. (1987). The Panda's Thumb of Technology. *Natural History*, 96 (1), 16–23.

8 Conclusions Regarding the Risk in Risk Management

1   Thompson, J. (1967). *Organizations in Action: Social Science Bases of Administrative Theory*. London: Transaction Publishers.

2   Mintzberg, H. (1979). *The Structuring of Organizations: A Synthesis of the Research*. Englewood Cliffs, NJ: Prentice Hall.

3   Greenwood, R. and Hinings, C. (1988). Design Archetypes, Tracks and the Dynamics of Strategic Change. *Organization Studies*, 9 (3), 293–316.

4   Miller, D. (1996). Configurations Revisited. *Strategic Management Journal*, 17 (7), 505–512.

5   Vit, G. (2007). The Multiple Logics of Conformity and Contrarianism: The Problem with Investment Banks and Bankers. *Journal of Management Inquiry*, 16 (3), 217–226.

6   Gimpl, M. and Dakin, S. (1984). Management and Magic. *California Management Review*, 27 (1), 125–136.

7   Staw, B. and Epstein, L. (2000). What Bandwagons Bring: Effects of Popular Management Techniques on Corporate Performance, Reputation, and CEO Pay. *Administrative Science Quarterly*, 45 (3), 523–556.

8   Galbraith, J. (2004). *The Economics of Innocent Fraud: Truth for Our Time*. New York: Houghton Mufflin Books.

9   Morison, E. (1966). Gunfire at Sea: A Case Study of Innovation. *Men, Machines and Modern Times*, Cambridge, MA: MIT Press, 17–44.

10 Phillips, N., Lawrence, T.B., and Hardy, C. (2004). Discourse and Institutions. *Academy of Management Review*, 29, 635–652.

11 Lawrence, T., Winn, M., and Jennings, P. (2001). The Temporal Dynamics of Institutionalization. *Academy of Management Review*, 26 (4), 624–645.

12 Lounsbury, M. (2007). The Tale of Two Cities: Competing Logics and Practice Variation in the Professionalizing of Mutual Funds' Forthcoming. *Academy of Management Journal*, 50 (2), 289–307.

13 Simon, H. (1979). Rational Decision Making in Business Organizations. *American Economic Review*, 69 (4), 495–513.

14 Mintzberg, H. (2004). *Managers Not MBAs: A Hard Look at the Soft Practice of Managing and Management Development*. San Francisco, CA: Berrett-Koehler Publishers, Inc.

15 For example, see Casualty Actuarial Society industry standard Enterprise Risk Management document May 2003, which highlights a SWOT model reminiscent of Fayol, H. (1916). *General and Industrial Management*. New York: Pitman, and Andrews (1965).

16 Gimpl and Dakin.

17 Galbraith.

18 Ansoff, H. (1965). *Corporate Strategy*. New York: McGraw-Hill, 923–952.

19 Andrews, K. ([1965] 1987). *The Concept of Corporate Strategy*. Homewood, IL: Dow Jones Irwin.

20 Wernerfelt, B. (1984). A Resource-Based View of the Firm. *Strategic Management Journal*, 5, 171–180.

21 Bill Starbuck has indicated 3.5 years on average.

22 Bhide, A. (1986). Hustle as Strategy. *Harvard Business Review*, 64, September.

23 Taylor, F.W. (1967). *The Principles of Scientific Management*. New York: Harper & Row.

24 Staw and Epstein.

25 ISO 13000 (13 November 2009). International Organization for Standardization. Retrieved from http://www.iso.org.

26 These have been raised by Mintzberg (1990) and Vit (2009) among others; see notes 27 and 28 below.

27 Vit, G. (2009). Foreseeing the Problem of Conformity and Contrarianism: The Problem with Investment Banks and Bankers. *Journal of Management Inquiry*, 16 (3), 217–226.

28 Mintzberg, H. (1990). Strategy Formation: Schools of Thought. In J. Fredrickson (ed.) *Perspectives on Strategic Management*. New York: Harper Business.

29 Vit, G. (1993). Canadian Bank Strategy: The CEO's Perspective. *CETAI Cahier de Recherche*, 93–18, Ecole des Hautes Etudes Commerciale, Montreal, Canada.

30 Staw and Epstein.

31 Clegg, S., Carter, C., and Kornberger, M. (2004). Get up, I Feel Like Being a Strategy Machine. *European Management Review*, 1, 21–28.

32 Merton, R.K. (1936). The Unanticipated Consequences of Purposive Social Action. *American Sociological Review*, 1 (6), 894–904.

33 Mintzberg, H. and Waters, J. (1985). Of Strategies, Deliberate and Emergent. *Strategic Management Journal*, 6 (3), 257–272.

34 Gimpl and Dakin.

35 Nonaka, I. (1994). A Dynamic Theory of Organizational Knowledge Creation. *Organization Science*, 5 (1), 14–37.

36 Pascale, R. (1984). Perspectives on Strategy: The Real Story behind Honda's Success. *California Management Review*, 26 (3), 47–72.

37 Hamel, G. (1990). *Leading the Revolution*. New York: Penguin Putnam Inc.

38 Anderson, P. and Tushman, M. (1991). Managing through Cycles of Technological Change. *Research Technology Management*, 34 (3), 26.

39 Fayol, H. (1916). *General and Industrial Management*. New York: Pitman.

40 Andrews, K. ([1965] 1987). *The Concept of Corporate Strategy*. Homewood, IL: Dow Jones Irwin.

41 Mintzberg (1990).

42 Martinet, A. (1999). La lecture stratégique du diagnostic global. In A. Marion (ed.) *Le diagnostic d'entreprise: Méthode et processus*. Paris: Economica.

43 Gosling, J. and Mintzberg, H. (2005). The Five Minds of a Manager. *Harvard Business Review*, 83, November.

44 Gimpl and Dakin.

45 Clegg et al..

46 Weick, K. (1979). *The Social Psychology of Organizing*. London: McGraw-Hill, Inc.

47 Shapira, Z. and Berndt, D. (1997). Managing Grand Scale Construction Projects: A Risk-Taking Perspective. *Research in Organizational Behaviour*, 19, 303–360.

48 Morison.

49 Gould, S. (1987). The Panda's Thumb of Technology. *Natural History*, 96 (1), 16–23.

50 Westley, F., Zimmerman, B., and Patton, M. (2007). *Getting to Maye How the World is Changed*. Toronto: Vintage Canada.

51 Vit, G. and Graham, J. (1997). Canada Changes Foreign Bank Laws. *Butterworth's Journal of International Banking and Financial Law*, September, 363–368.

52 Vit, G. (1996). Financial Services Industry Mismanagement: Institutionalization and Conformist Strategy. *International Journal of Service Industry Management*, 7 (3), 6–16.

53 Simon, H. (1945). *Administrative Behavior*. New York: The Free Press.

54 Vickers, G. (1965). *The Art of Judgment: A Study of Policy Making*. London: Chapman and Hall.

55 Strebel, P. (1992). *Breakpoints: How Managers Exploit Radical Business Change*. Boston, MA: Harvard Business School Press.

56 Bronowski, J. (1958). The Creative Process. *Scientific American*, 199 (3), Sept., 59–65.

57 Quinn, J.B., Anderson, P., and Finklestein, S. (1996). Managing Professional Intellect. *Harvard Business Review*, 74, 71–80.

58 Miller, D. (1987). The Genesis of Configuration. *Academy of Management Review*, 12 (4), 686–701.

59 Miller (1996).

60 Greenwood, R. and Hinings, C. (1993). Understanding Strategic Change: The Contribution of Archetypes. *Academy of Management Journal*, 36 (5), 1052–1081.

61 Thompson.

62 Mintzberg, H. (1991). The Effective Organization: Forces and Forms. *Sloan Management Review*, 32 (2), 57–67.

63 Zald, M. and Denton, P. (1963). From Evangelism to General Service: The Transformation of the YMCA. *Administrative Science Quarterly*, 8 (2), 214–234.

64 Meyer, J. and Rowan, B. (1977). Institutionalized Organizations: Formal Structures as Myth and Ceremony. *American Journal of Sociology*, 83 (2), 340–363.

65 DiMaggio, P. and Powell, M. (1983). The Iron Cage Revisited: Institutional Isomorphism and Collective Rationality in Organizational Fields. *American Sociological Review*, 48 (2), 147–160.

66 Scott, W. (1995). *Institutions and Organizations*. London: Sage Publications.

67 Holm, P. (1995). The Dynamics of Institutionalization: Transformation Processes in Norwegian Fisheries. *Administrative Science Quarterly*, 40 (30), 398–422.

68 Vit (2007).

69 Pfeffer, J. (1993). Barriers to the Advancement of Organizational Science: Paradigm Development as a Dependent Variable. *American Management Review*, 18 (4), 599–620.

70 Vit, G. (2006). Organizational Conformity and Contrarianism: Regular Irregular Trading at National Australia Bank. *Corporate Governance*, 6 (2), 203–214.

71 Minsky, H.P. (1972). Financial Stability Revisited: The Economics of Disaster. *Board of Governors of the Federal Reserve System: Reappraisal of the Federal Reserve Discount Mechanism*, 3, 95–136.

72 Kindleberger, C. (1978). *Manias, Panics and Crashes: A History of Financial Crises*. New York: Basic Books.

73 Merton, R.K. (1938). Social Structure and Anomie. *American Sociological Review*, 3 (5), 672–682.

74 Morison.

75 Mintzberg (2004).

76 Christensen, C., Craig, T., and Hart, S. (2001). The Great Disruption. *Foreign Affairs*, 80 (2), 80–95.

77 Joy, W. (2000). Why the Future Doesn't Need Us. *Wired*, 8 April, 1–12.

78 Bird, K. and Sherwin, M.J. (2005). *American Prometheus: The Triumph and Tragedy of J. Robert Oppenheimer*. New York: Random House Digital, Inc.

79 Allison, G. (2005). *Nuclear Terrorism: The Ultimate Preventable Catastrophe*. New York: Henry Holt.

Works Cited

Abolafia, M. and Kilduff, M. (1988). Enacting Market Crisis: The Social Construction of a Speculative Bubble. *Administrative Science Quarterly*, 33 (2), 177–193.

Abrahamson, E. and Fairchild, G. (1999). Management Fashion: Lifecycles, Triggers, and Collective Learning Processes. *Administrative Science Quarterly*, 44 (4), 708–740.

Achbar, M. and Wintonick, P. (1992). *Manufacturing Consent: Noam Chomsky and the Media*, documentary film, National Film Board of Canada, Montreal.

Aldrich, H. and Ruef, M. (1999). *Organizations Evolving*. Thousand Oaks, CA: Sage Publications.

Allison, G. (1971). *The Essence of Decision: Explaining the Cuban Missile Crisis*. London: Little Brown and Co.

Allison, G. (2005). *Nuclear Terrorism: The Ultimate Preventable Catastrophe*. New York: Henry Holt.

Alvesson, M. (1991). Organizational Symbolism and Ideology. *Journal of Management Studies*, 28 (3), 207–225.

Anderson, P., and Tushman, M. (1991). Managing through Cycles of Technological Change. *Research Technology Management*, 34 (3), 26.

Andrews, K. ([1965] 1987). *The Concept of Corporate Strategy*. Homewood, IL: Dow Jones Irwin.

Ansoff, H. (1965). *Corporate Strategy*. New York: McGraw-Hill, 923–952.

Ashforth, B.E. and Mael, F. (1989). Social Identity Theory and the Organization. *Academy of Management Review*, 14 (1), 20–39.

Asquith, P., Mullins, J., and Wolff, E.D. (1989). Original Issue High Yield Bonds: Aging Analyses of Defaults, Exchanges, and Calls. *Journal of Finance*, 44 (September), 923–952.

Australian Prudential Regulation Authority (2004). *Report into Irregular Currency Options Trading at the National Australia Bank*. Sydney: Commonwealth of Australia, 5.

Baker, P.L. (1987). Banking Transformed: Women's Work and Technological Change in a Canadian Bank. Unpublished PhD thesis, University of Toronto, Canada.

Bank of Canada (1983). *Bank of Canada Review*. Ottawa: Bank of Canada.

Bank of Canada (1987). Text of a speech given by John W. Crow, Governor of the Bank of Canada, to the 71st Annual Meeting of the Investment Dealers' Association of Canada, Ottawa, June 9.

Barigazzi, J. (2004). Parmalat's Ex-Finance Chief Blames Boss. *Globe and Mail*, June 1.

Bhide, A. (1986). Hustle as Strategy. *Harvard Business Review*, 64, September.

Bird, K. and Sherwin, M.J. (2005). *American Prometheus: The Triumph and Tragedy of J. Robert Oppenheimer*. New York: Random House Digital, Inc.

Brealey, R. (1985). *An Introduction to Risk and Return*. London: Blackwell.

Bronowski, J. (1958). The creative process. *Scientific American*, 199 (3), Sept., 59–65.

Brunsson, N. (1982). The Irrationality of Action and Action Rationality: Decisions, Ideologies and Organizational Actions. *Journal of Management Studies*, 19 (1), 29–44.

Bullen, D. (2004). *Fake: My Life as a Rogue Trader*. Mississauga: Wiley.

Butler, R. (1991). *Designing Organizations: A Decision-Making Perspective*. London: Routledge.

Christensen, C., Craig, T., and Hart, S. (2001). The Great Disruption. *Foreign Affairs*, 80 (2), 80–95.

Clegg, S., Carter, C., and Kornberger, M. (2004). Get Up, I Feel Like Being a Strategy Machine. *European Management Review*, 1 (1), 21–28.

Covaleski, M. and Dirsmith, M. (1988). An Institutional Perspective on the Rise, Social Transformation, and Fall of a University Budget Category. *Administrative Science Quarterly*, 13 (4), 562–587.

Cray, D. and Colignon, R. (1980). Critical Organizations. *Organizational Studies*, 1 (4), 349–365.

Darroch, J. (1990). Canadian Bank Strategy. Unpublished PhD thesis, York University, Canada.

Darroch, J. and Litvach, A. (1991). Canadian Banks: Strategic Initiatives. *Business Quarterly*, Autumn.

DiMaggio, P. and Powell, M. (1983). The Iron Cage Revisited: Institutional Isomorphism and Collective Rationality in Organizational Fields. *American Sociological Review*, 48 (2), 147–160.

DiMaggio, P. and Powell, W. (1991). *The New Institutionalism in Organizational Analysis*. Chicago, IL: University of Chicago Press.

Dobson, W. (2004). Parmalat's Babcock Institute Discussion Paper No. 2004-4. Madison, WI: The Babcock Institute for International Dairy Research and Development.

Elsbach, K. (1999). An Expanded Model of Organizational Identification. In R. Sutton and B. M. Staw (eds.) *Research in Organizational Behaviour*, 21. London: JAI Press, 163–200.

Fayol, H. (1916). *General and Industrial Management*. New York: Pitman.

Fédération des travailleurs du Québec (n.d.). Retrieved from http://ftq.qc.ca/.

Feldman, M. and Pentland, B. (2003). Reconceptualizing Organizational Routines as a Source of Flexibility and Change. *Administrative Science Quarterly*, 48 (1), 94–118.

Ferrari, U., Brocklehurst, C., and Wright, A. (2002). Tulips, railways and telecom. *UBS Warbug Global Equity Research*, 1–41.

Financial Crisis Inquiry Report (2011) *Final Report of the National Commission on the Causes of the Financial and Economic Crisis in the United States.* New York: US Government Printing Office.

Galbraith, J.K. (2004). *The Economics of Innocent Fraud.* New York: Houghton Mifflin Company.

Geertz, R. (1973). *Notes on the Balinese Cockfight in the Interpretation of Cultures.* New York: Basic Books.

Gimpl, M. and Dakin, S. (1984). Management and Magic. *California Management Review,* 27 (1), 125–136.

Golden-Biddle, K. and Hayagreeva, R. (1997). Breaches in the Boardroom: Organizational Identity and Conflicts of Commitment in a Non-profit Organization. *Organization Science,* 8 (6), 593–611.

Goldstone, J. (Producer) and Jones, T. (Director) (1979). *Monty Python's Life of Brian.* United Kingdom: Cinema International Corporation.

Gosling, J. and Mintzberg, H. (2005). The Five Minds of a Manager. *Harvard Business Review,* 83, November.

Gould, S. (1987). The Panda's Thumb of Technology. *Natural History,* 96 (1), 16–23.

Greenwood, R. and Hinings, C. (1988). Design Archetypes, Tracks and the Dynamics of Strategic Change. *Organization Studies,* 9 (3), 293–316.

Greenwood, R. and Hinings, C. (1993). Understanding Strategic Change: The Contribution of Archetypes. *Academy of Management Journal,* 36 (5), 1052–1081.

Hamel, G. (1990). *Leading the Revolution.* New York: Penguin Putnam Inc.

Hofstede, G. (1990). Motivation, Leadership, and Organizations: Do American Theories Apply Abroad? *Organizational Dynamics,* 19 (Summer).

Holm, P. (1995). The Dynamics of Institutionalization: Transformation Processes in Norwegian Fisheries. *Administrative Science Quarterly,* 40 (3), 398–422.

Hurst, D. (1986). Why Strategic Management Is Bankrupt. *Organizational Dynamics,* 15 (2), 5–27.

ISO 13000 (13 November 2009). International Organization for Standardization. Retrieved from http://www.iso.org.

Jaeger, A. and Kanungo, R. (1990). Management in Developing Countries. *Strategic Management Journal,* 9, 31–41.

Joy, W. (2000). Why the Future Doesn't Need Us. *Wired,* 8 April, 1–12.

Keil, M. (1995). Pulling the Plug: Software Project Management and the Problem of Project Escalation. *MIS Quarterly,* 19(4), 421–447.

Kindleberger, C. (1978). *Manias, Panics and Crashes: A History of Financial Crises.* New York: Basic Books.

Kondratieff, N.D. and Stolper, W.F. (1935). The Long Waves in Economic Life. *Review of Economic Statistics,* 17 (6), 105–115.

KPMG (2008). *Letter of Substantiation in Report to Shareholders on UBS Writedowns.* Zurich.

La Société générale de financement (2001). Gaspesia Mill to Reopen. Montreal, Quebec, Canada, December 17.

La Société générale de financement (2002). SGF: Regional Investments Bearing Fruit in the

Gaspé and Magdalen Islands: $550 Million Invested with Partners over 1,200 Jobs Created. Montreal, Quebec, Canada, May 2.

La Société générale de financement (2003). SGF Tables Its 2002 Annual Report at the National Assembly. Montreal, Quebec, Canada, June 12.

La Société générale de financement (2004). GF Continues to Support the Administrator's Efforts to Revive Gaspésia. Montréal, Quebec, Canada, September 23.

La Société générale de financement (2004). Papiers Gaspésia obtient une prorogation de la cour de quarante jours. Montreal, Quebec, Canada, February 27.

Lawrence, T., Winn, M., and Jennings, P. (2001). The Temporal Dynamics of Institutionalization. *Academy of Management Review*, 26 (4), 624–645.

Lesage, R. (2005). Rapport d'enquête sur les dépassements de coûts et de délais du chantier de la Société Papiers Gaspésia de Chandler / Commission d'enquête sur la Société Papiers Gaspésia. Québec: Commission d'enquête sur la Société Papiers Gaspésia. Quebec, Canada.

Lounsbury, M. (2007). The Tale of Two Cities: Competing Logics and Practice Variation in the Professionalizing of Mutual Funds' Forthcoming. *Academy of Management Journal*, 50 (2), 289–307.

Lounsbury, M. and Hirsch, P. (2010). Markets on Trial: Toward a Policy-Oriented Economic Sociology. *Markets on Trial: The Economic Sociology of the U.S. Financial Crisis*, Research in the Sociology of Organizations 30. Bingley: Emerald.

MacIntosh, R. (1991). *Different Drummers: Banking and Politics in Canada*. Toronto: Macmillan of Canada.

MacKay, C. (1914). *Memoirs of Extraordinary Popular Delusions and the Madness of Crowds*, reprinted ed. (1932). Boston: L.C. Page Co.

McNamara, G., Moon, H., and Bronmiley, P. (2002). Banking on Commitment: Intended and Unintended Consequences of an Organization's Attempt to Attenuate Escalation of Commitment. *Academy of Management Journal*, 45 (2), 443–452.

Maguire, S. (2003). The Co-evolution of Technology and Discourse: A Study of Substitution Processes for the Insecticide DDT. *Organization Studies*, 25(1), 113–134.

Marsden, D. (1991). Indigenous Management. *Journal of Human Resource Management*, 2 (1).

Martinet, A. (1999). La lecture stratégique du diagnostic global. In A. Marion (ed.) *Le diagnostic d'entreprise: Méthode et processus*. Paris: Economica.

Mello, A., Attari, M., and Ruckes, M. (2003). Arbitraging Arbitrageurs. *Journal of Finance*, 60 (5), 2471–2511.

Merton, R.C. (1973). Theory of Rational Option Pricing. *Bell Journal of Economics and Management Science*, 4, 141–183.

Merton, R.K. (1936). The Unanticipated Consequences of Purposive Social Action. *American Sociological Review*, 1 (6), 894–904.

Merton, R.K. (1938). Social Structure and Anomie. *American Sociological Review*, 3 (5), 672–682.

Meyer, J. and Rowan, B. (1977). Institutionalized Organizations: Formal Structures as Myth and Ceremony. *American Journal of Sociology*, 83 (2), 340–363.

Meyer, J., Rowan, B., Deal, T., and Scott, W. (1983). *Organizational Environments: Ritual and Rationality.* London: Sage Publications.

Michaels, A. (2004). Court Grants Parmalat Claims. *Financial Times*, Dec. 17.

Miller, C., Cardinal, L., and Glick, W. (1997). Retrospective Reports in Organizational Research. *Academy of Management Journal*, 40 (1), 189–204.

Miller, D. (1987). The Genesis of Configuration. *Academy of Management Review*, 12 (4), 686–701.

Miller, D. (1993). The Architecture of Simplicity. *Academy of Management Review*, 18 (1), 116–138.

Miller, D. (1996). Configurations Revisited. *Strategic Management Journal*, 17 (7), 505–512.

Miller, R. and Lessard, D. (2000). *The Strategic Management of Large Engineering Projects.* Cambridge, MA: MIT.

Minsky, H.P. (1972). Financial Stability Revisited: The Economics of Disaster. *Board of Governors of the Federal Reserve System, Reappraisal of the Federal Reserve Discount Mechanism*, 3, 95–136.

Mintzberg, H. (1979). *The Structuring of Organizations: A Synthesis of the Research.* Englewood Cliffs, NJ: Prentice Hall.

Mintzberg, H. (1983). *Structure in Fives: Designing Effective Organizations.* Englewood Cliffs, NJ: Prentice Hall.

Mintzberg, H. (1990). Strategy Formation: Schools of Thought. In J. Fredrickson (ed.) *Perspectives on Strategic Management.* New York: Harper Business.

Mintzberg, H. (1991). The Effective Organization: Forces and Forms. *Sloan Management Review*, 32 (2), 57–67.

Mintzberg, H. (1994). The Fall and Rise of Strategic Planning. *Harvard Business Review*, 72, Jan./Feb.

Mintzberg, H. (2004). *Managers Not MBAs: A Hard Look at the Soft Practice of Managing and Management Development.* San Francisco, CA: Berrett-Koehler Publishers, Inc.

Mintzberg, H. and Waters, J. (1985). Of Strategies, Deliberate and Emergent. *Strategic Management Journal*, 6 (3), 257–272.

Morison, E. (1966). Gunfire at Sea: A Case Study of Innovation. In E. Morison (ed.) *Men, Machines and Modern Times.* Cambridge, MA: MIT Press, 17–44.

Mortensen, M. and Hinds, P. (2002). Fuzzy Teams: Boundary Disagreement in Distributed and Collocated Teams. In P. Hinds and S. Kiesler (eds.) *Distributed Work.* Cambridge, MA: MIT Press, pp. 281–308.

National Australia Bank (n.d.). Retrieved from http://www.nab.com.au/.

Nelson, R. (1991). How Do Firms Differ and Why Does It Matter? *Strategic Management Journal*, 12 (2), 61–74.

Nonaka, I. (1994). A Dynamic Theory of Organizational Knowledge Creation. *Organization Science*, 5 (1), 14–37.

Nowzad, B. (1990). Lessons of the Debt Debacle. *Finance and Development*, 27 (March), 9–13.

Ocasio, W. (1997). Towards an Attention Based View of the Firm. *Strategic Management Journal*, 18 (1), 187–206.

Oliver, C. (1991). Strategic Responses to Organizational Processes. *Academy of Management Review*, 16 (1), 145–179.

Oliver, C. (1992). The Antecedents of Deinstitutionalization. *Organization Studies*, 13 (4), 563–588.

Oxford Dictionary of English (2005, 2nd ed.). Oxford: Oxford University Press.

Palmer, D. and Maher, M.W. (2010). A Normal Accident Analysis of the Mortgage Meltdown. In M. Lounsbury and P. Hirsch (eds.) *Markets on Trial: The Economic Sociology of the U.S. Financial Crisis*, Research in the Sociology of Organizations 30. Bingley: Emerald.

Parmalat S.p.A. Sede (2003). *Parmalat*. Retrieved from http://www.parmalat.com/en/.

Pascale, R. (1984). Perspectives on Strategy: The Real Story behind Honda's Success. *California Management Review*, 26 (3), 47–72.

Pascale, R. (1990). *Managing on the Edge: How the Smartest Companies Use Conflict to Stay Ahead*. New York: Simon & Schuster.

Perrow, C. (2010). The Meltdown Was Not an Accident. In M. Lounsbury and P. Hirsch (eds.) *Markets on Trial: The Economic Sociology of the U.S. Financial Crisis*, Research in the Sociology of Organizations 30. Bingley: Emerald, pp. 309–330.

Pettigrew, A. (1992). The Character and Significance of Strategy Process Research. *Strategic Management Journal*, 13, 5–16.

Pfeffer, J. (1982). *Organizations and Organization Theory*. London: Pitman.

Pfeffer, J. (1993). Barriers to the Advancement of Organizational Science: Paradigm Development as a Dependent Variable. *Academy of Management Review*, 18 (4), 599–620.

Pfeffer, J. and Salancik, G. (1978). *The External Control of Organizations: A Resource Dependence Perspective*. New York: Harper & Row.

Phillips, N., Lawrence, T.B., and Hardy, C. (2004). Discourse and Institutions. *Academy of Management Review*, 29, 635–652.

PricewaterhouseCoopers (2008). Société Générale: Summary of PwC Diagnostic Review and Analysis of the Action Plan. Paris, p. 6.

Quinn, J.B., Anderson, P., and Finklestein, S. (1996). Managing Professional Intellect. *Harvard Business Review*, 74, 71–80.

Ramanujam, R. and Goodman, P. (2003). Latent Errors and Adverse Organizational Consequences: A Conceptualization. *Journal of Organizational Behaviour*, 24 (7), 815–836.

Ross, J. and Staw, B. (1993). Organizational Escalation and Exit: Lessons from the Shoreham Nuclear Power Plant. *Academy of Management Journal*, 36 (4), 701–732.

Schein, E. (1983). The Role of the Founder in Creating Organizational Culture. *Organizational Dynamics*, 12 (1), 13–28.

Schwartz, N. and Bennhold, K. (2008). In France, the Heads No Longer Roll. *New York Times*, February 17.

Scott, W. (1995). *Institutions and Organizations*. London: Sage Publications.

Seegar, J. (1984). Research Notes and Communication: Reversing the Images of BCG's Growth/Share Matrix. *Strategic Management Journal*, 5, 93–97.

Selznick, P. (1957). *Leadership in Administration: A Sociological Interpretation*. London: Harper & Row.

Shapira, Z. and Berndt, D. (1997). Managing Grand Scale Construction Projects: A Risk-Taking Perspective. *Research in Organizational Behaviour*, 19, 303–360.

Simon, H. (1945). *Administrative Behavior*. New York: Macmillan.

Simon, H. (1979). Rational Decision Making in Business Organizations. *American Economic Review*, 69 (4), 495–513.

Smith, A. (1776). *An Inquiry into the Nature and Causes of the Wealth of Nations*. London: Methuen & Co., Ltd.

Smith, M. (2005). The Parmalat Syndrome. *SF Weekly*, January 12.

Société Générale (2007a). 2007 Registration Document. Paris: Tour Société Générale, 125–151.

Société Générale (2007b). Report of the Special Committee of the Board of Directors to the General Shareholders Meeting. Paris.

Société Générale (2008a). General Inspection Department: Mission Green Summary Report. Paris: Tour Société Générale.

Société Générale. (2008b). Progress Report of the Special Committee of the Board of Directors. Paris.

Spender, J. (1993). Some Frontier Activities around Strategy Theorizing. *Journal of Management Studies*, 30 (1), 11–29.

Srinivas, N. (1992). Indigenous Management. *CETAI Cahier de Recherche*, 92-16, Ecole des Hautes Etudes Commerciales, Montreal, Canada.

Staw, B.M. (1981). The Escalation of Commitment to a Course of Action. *Academy of Management Review*, 6 (4), 577–587.

Staw, B.M. and Epstein, L. (2000). What Bandwagons Bring: Effects of Popular Management Techniques on Corporate Performance, Reputation, and CEO Pay. *Administrative Science Quarterly*, 45 (3), 523–556.

Strebel, P. (1992). *Breakpoints: How Managers Exploit Radical Business Change*. Boston, MA: Harvard Business School Press.

Suddaby, R. and Greenwood, R. (2005). Rhetorical Strategies of Legitimacy. *Administrative Science Quarterly*, 50 (1), 35–67.

Sylvers, E. (2005). Parmalat Trial in Milan Nets 11 Convictions. *International Herald Tribune*, June 29.

Taylor, F.W. (1967). *The Principles of Scientific Management*. New York: Harper & Row.

Tembec, Inc. (2000). Tembec Financial Report 2000, p. 2.

Tembec (2004). Tembec to Write Down Its Investment in Gaspesia Papers. Quebec, Canada, February 25.

Thompson, J. (1967). *Organizations in Action: Social Science Bases of Administrative Theory*. New York: McGraw-Hill.

Thompson, J. and Tudon, A. (1959). Strategies, Structure, and Processes of Organizational Decision. In J. Thompson, P.B. Iammond, R.W. Hawkes, and A. Tudon (eds.) *Comparative Studies in Administration*. Pittsburgh, PA: University of Pittsburgh Press.

UBS (2008a). *20 F Filing to United States Securities and Exchange Commission*. Washington, D.C.

UBS (2008b). *Shareholder Report on UBS's Writedowns*. Zurich.

UBS (2009a). *10 F Filing to United States Securities and Exchange Commission.* Washington, D.C.

UBS (2009b). *UBS Results in First Quarter 2009.* Zurich.

UBS (2009c). *UBS Results in Fourth Quarter 2008.* Zurich.

United States of America, Financial Crisis Inquiry Commission. (2011). *The Financial Crisis Inquiry Report,* commissioned by Angelides, P., Thomas, B., Born, B., Murren, H.H., Graham, B. et al. Washington: U.S. Government Printing Office.

Vickers, G. (1965). *The Art of Judgment: A Study of Policy Making.* London: Chapman and Hall.

Vit, G. (1993). Canadian Bank Strategy: The CEO's Perspective. *CETAI Cahier de Recherche,* 93-18, Ecole des Hautes Etudes Commerciale, Montreal, Canada.

Vit, G. (1996). Financial Services Industry Mismanagement: Institutionalization and Conformist Strategy. *International Journal of Service Industry Management,* 7 (3), 6–16.

Vit, G. (2006). Organizational Conformity and Contrarianism: Regular Irregular Trading at National Australia Bank. *Corporate Governance,* 6 (2), 203–214.

Vit, G. (2007). The Multiple Logics of Conformity and Contrarianism: The Problem with Investment Banks and Bankers. *Journal of Management Inquiry,* 16 (3), 217–226.

Vit, G. (2009). Foreseeing the Problem of Conformity in Strategy Teaching, Research and Practice. In B. MacKay and L. Constanza (eds.) *The Handbook of Research on Strategy and Foresight.* Northampton, MA: Edward Elgar Publishing Limited, pp. 518–527.

Vit, G. (2010). Competing Logics: Project Failure in Gaspesia. *European Management Journal,* 29 (3), 234–244.

Vit, G. and Graham, J. (1997). Canada Changes Foreign Bank Laws. *Butterworth's Journal of International Banking and Financial Law,* September, 363–368.

Weick, K. (1979). *The Social Psychology of Organizing.* London: McGraw-Hill.

Wernerfelt, B. (1984). A Resource-Based View of the Firm. *Strategic Management Journal,* 5, 171–180.

Westley, F. and Bird, F. (1990). The Sociology of Organizational Commitment: A Comparative Review of Classical Theories. Working Paper, McGill University.

Westley, F., Zimmerman, B., and Patton, M. (2007). *Getting to Maybe How the World is Changed.* Toronto: Vintage Canada.

Zajac, E. and Westphal, J. (2004). The Social Construction of Market Value Institutionalization and Learning Perspectives on Stock Market Reactions. *American Sociological Review,* 69(3), 433–457.

Zald, M. and Denton, P. (1963). From Evangelism to General Service: The Transformation of the YMCA. *Administrative Science Quarterly,* 8 (2), 214–234.

Zucker, L. (1987). Institutional Theories of Organization. *Annual Review of Sociology,* 13, 443–464.

Index

Taylor & Francis
eBooks
FOR LIBRARIES

ORDER YOUR FREE 30 DAY INSTITUTIONAL TRIAL TODAY!

Over 23,000 eBook titles in the Humanities, Social Sciences, STM and Law from some of the world's leading imprints.

Choose from a range of subject packages or create your own!

Benefits for **you**

▶ Free MARC records
▶ COUNTER-compliant usage statistics
▶ Flexible purchase and pricing options

Benefits for your **user**

▶ Off-site, anytime access via Athens or referring URL
▶ Print or copy pages or chapters
▶ Full content search
▶ Bookmark, highlight and annotate text
▶ Access to thousands of pages of quality research at the click of a button

For more information, pricing enquiries or to order a free trial, contact your local online sales team.

UK and Rest of World: **online.sales@tandf.co.uk**
US, Canada and Latin America:
e-reference@taylorandfrancis.com

www.ebooksubscriptions.com

Taylor & Francis eBooks
Taylor & Francis Group

ALPSP Award for BEST eBOOK PUBLISHER 2009 Finalist

A flexible and dynamic resource for teaching, learning and research.